THE FUN OF REFINISHING
FURNITURE FROM A TO Z

The Fun of Refinishing Furniture from A to Z

By that master of Yankee wit & wisdom

GEORGE GROTZ

Revealing some new tricks of the
trade, more about his Infamous Uncle George
—plus 59 illustrations by the author,
and *one* by Leonardo da Vinci!

A DOLPHIN BOOK
Doubleday & Company, Inc.
Garden City, New York
1979

ISBN: 0-385-14916-6
Library of Congress Catalog Card Number 78–22809

Preface

Hello Out There—Again!

Or, are you really ready to go another round with The Furniture Doctor?

My wife says I ought to stop writing these books about furniture refinishing. She says I've already made my point in the first seven of them. But I can't seem to break the habit. The habit of eating, that is. And writing books sure beats working for a living.

But to tell the truth, I think I'm getting better at it all the time. I think this is the best one I ever did. Maybe a masterpiece. And anyway if you don't like it you don't have to buy it. It's still a free country, last I heard. Especially here in Massachusetts. We moved down here from Vermont about ten years ago. One day I was out in the woodshed after being snowed in for five days, and it was so cold I could hear my skull cracking as it contracted. So as I stood there looking out the window at all that snow—all just different colors of white—I said to myself, "I may not be the smartest fellow in the world, but I ain't dumb enough to go through another one of these damn Vermont winters."

Of course, that doesn't have much to do with telling you what this book is all about. I mean, why another one? Well, this time I have tried to relate repair and refinishing techniques specifically to each of over fifty styles and special pieces of furniture. And also to the different kinds of wood found in furniture. In other words, it's a sort of dictionary, as opposed to a handbook. That's why we almost called it "Refinishing Reconsidered," but that sounded a little too high-brow.

But if you still don't get my pitch, why don't you just look at the table of contents. That will give you the picture pretty fast, and I'll be able to knock off work (?) early today. Which I'd really like to do. You see, I've got a date with a good looking granddaughter. She's almost four, and this afternoon we're going to build a milk truck together.

You stick together, too.

George Grotz
Massachusetts, 1974

Contents

Which you are going to have to learn to live with if you are going to make any sense out of this book at all.

Part I
BASIC THINGS TO KNOW

A quick review of the tricks and techniques
that we will be referring back to from our much
more interesting Part II.

Part II
HOW TO DO IT FROM A TO Z

Being an alphabetical approach to
the specific problems you will run into,
plus a few you'd love to have.

Part III
MORE ABOUT MY INFAMOUS UNCLE GEORGE
(And My Aunt Mary, too!)

Appendix

Part I

Basic Things to Know

A quick review of the tricks and techniques that we will be referring back to from our much more interesting Part II.

1

What Wood Is Like

How the characteristics of the different woods
determines the ways you can repair them, stain them
and finish them—and why they were used to make what!

I hate to be the kind of fellow that asks you to get down
to fundamentals first. It's always so much more fun to
rush in where angels fear to tread and make a big mess.
Which can also be a good learning process. But I've gotten pretty fond of wood over the years, so I think I'll
take a shot at getting you interested in it, too.

To begin with, wood doesn't really have pores. But it
does look like it does, so later on you'll probably catch
me using the term myself. It communicates. But wood is
actually made of a lot of little hollow tubes. When you
think about it, it would have to be to carry the water up
to the leaves. Some trip in a redwood tree!

Now in some woods these tubes are large and straight.
In others they are tiny and twisty, which is what makes
some woods hard to split with an ax. And there are all

kinds of variations of sizes and shapes of tubes which give different woods different characteristics when it comes to cutting them, staining them, bleaching them, sanding them and putting a finish on them. All of which have an influence on which woods are used for furniture. So here are some descriptions of woods that have ended up being used in furniture over the years.

OAK is a very hard wood of a pale yellow color but brittle and splintery in its hardness. If you ever tried to work it with hand tools after it has aged a couple of decades, you might think it was made out of iron. That is why it didn't come into common use for furniture until woodworking machinery came along, and then bango you got all your Victorian Oak. It was as if man was getting back at all the oak trees for being so hard all the years up to then.

Because it is so hard, stain won't sink into its fibres or tubes to color it. Except for the giant tubes about a thirty-second of an inch apart that give oak its characteristic look of having "pores." These are the ends of the big tubes cut across at an angle. The apparently solid areas between these "pores" are just made up of tubes so tiny you need a microscope to see them.

WHITE PINE, to try to make this a little interesting, lies at the other end of the hardness scale of wood. This is the tall pine with needles instead of leaves that grows in northern or high mountain places. And because of its tube structure it turns out to be very light and soft, which makes it easy to cut and not very likely to splinter (but not perfect). However its soft porosity makes it just about perfect for staining it any color. This is because its tubes are relatively large for sucking stain into themselves well, but well below a size that can be seen with the naked eye.

At this point let's squelch any confusion about the kinds of pine. *Some* pines (also complete with needles instead of leaves) are very hard. These are the tall straight trees that grow in hot southern climates and make good telephone poles. But the wood is very hard and splintery. Or soft with streaks of hard, which is as bad as you can get for both cutting and staining. Cheap plywood is made of thin slices of this peeled off by a blade running the full length of a revolving log. The most generally used name for this family of southern pines is YELLOW PINE. But if you say "southern pine" to anybody in the wood business, you will have made your point.

So there is a very strong wood (oak), but so hard you need machines to cut it, and an easy cutting, stainable wood (pine), which is too weak to make chair legs out of it and so soft that it easily dents on the bottoms of legs and tabletop edges. So for general use cabinet-makers have always looked for some wood in between them that would have the desirable characteristics of both: strong, but not too hard, non-splintering, able to take stain, pretty figures, etc. And what they found, of course, are the historically preferred cabinet woods. (By "historically" I refer to the last three hundred years of European and American craftsmanship in furniture and other wooden artifacts. Anything before that has either turned to dust or is in a museum where you'll never get your hands on it. And I don't see any point in my looking up the names of comparable Chinese and Indian and Siamese woods and so forth. There are thousands of kinds of woods around the continents of the world, so anything we are talking about will be matched by some other wood everywhere. Well, maybe not in the Antarctic.)

So what are the preferred cabinet woods? As it has turned out, they are:

WALNUT
FRUITWOOD
HONDURAS MAHOGANY
AMERICAN CHERRY

First came the walnuts and fruit tree woods that grew in northern Italy and southern France at the beginning of our historical era. Then as world trade got going England began bringing in Honduras mahogany to add to these two. And in the early years of the United States we found a very nice American walnut, and as a substitute for the reddish Honduras mahogany the English wouldn't let us have any of, we found our own terrific cherry.

What all these woods have in common is:

A reasonable degree of strength.

They are not too hard to be worked with hand tools.

You can carve them easily because they tend to splinter.

They absorb stains well and evenly.

The areas of their limb crotches and bulbous bases can be sliced into thin veneers that contain interesting convoluted figures that can be accented by staining.

Finally, a few things I left out of the above discourse to keep the ball rolling while I had it going.

PUMPKIN PINE. You see this term a lot in advertisements, but it doesn't really mean anything. Supposedly it comes from white pine trees that grew up in swamps and has a slight orange cast, especially around its knots. Well, maybe so, but not much pine gets cut down in swamps. And the people who talk about it the most are actually using white pine and giving it a pale orange stain.

EARLY AMERICAN PINE. I said that when they got to America the cabinetmakers found good American-brand walnuts and cherry wood. So what about the pine? Well, the thing is that the fine craftsmen didn't use it because of its excessive softness. The pine furniture was made by the farmers themselves in their slow winter months. And

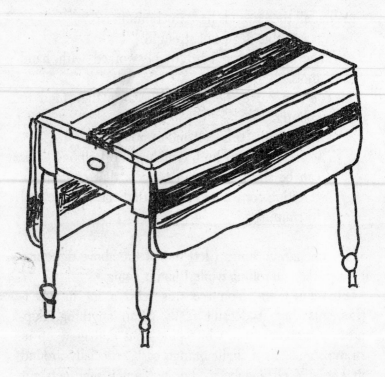

In this exquisite drawing obviously done for me by
Leonardo da Vinci, we have your basic imitation cherry
table made out of poplar—a tree that has a green core,
and so provides green streaks in the middle of tops and
leaves. However, the drawing exaggerates. And the rest
of the wood does look just like cherry when stained
brown mahogany, or just a little more orangy. Then by
wiping some extra opaque oil stains into the streaks, you
can almost conceal them and fool a lot of people.

then later on it was made by the small-town carpenters in their slow winter months, and eventually some of these went into it full time and became small-town cabinetmakers, as they are usually called. And this explains why you can find such a thing as a pine Chippendale chair. What happened was that as these country cabinetmakers became more sophisticated they began making imitations in their pine of the stuff they had seen done by English cabinetmakers in the cities—or for that matter, imported from England. (Let none of the above be misunderstood to mean that I am knocking Early American pine furniture. It is about the best example in the history of art of the beautiful results of functionalism in design. But it sure broke, wore out and rotted easily. For the last, especially witness the missing feet of all pine tavern tables because they stood on dirt floors.)

MAPLE. I know that there are some early maple things, but the reason there was so little is that it was too hard to work. About the only thing the early fellows felt it was reasonable to do with it was put it in a lathe—the earliest of woodworking machines—and make bed posts out of it. So you do find it in "cannonball" and tester bed posts.

The commercially popular Colonial Maple reproductions are not only an abortion in design, they are a reproduction of something that never existed—the ultimate monstrosity made like Frankenstein's monster in

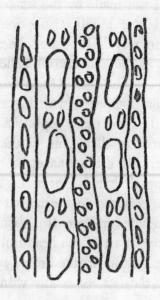

When you magnify a cross section—the end grain—of a piece of wood you get something like this. Thousands of tiny tubes ready to suck in stain. When wood that has twisty and curvy tubes is cut so that some of the tubes are cut off on the flat surface, then you have your so-called "pores."

But the real problem is that the end of a plank of wood will stain up much darker than the side surface. The solution is to seal the ends with shellac before applying your stain. Too much stain can easily be removed with alcohol to get the right balance.

response to the complete fugality of the taste of the American common man. Lincoln can have them!

BROWN MAHOGANY. This modern figureless veneer which is also so popular with the sons and daughters of the American immigrant classes is another of my least favorite vulgarisms. To begin with, it is no more mahogany than I am. What happened was that the Honduras mahogany ran out. So the big operators in the mass production furniture business found a lot of trees of easy-working, easy-staining wood in the Philippines and Africa and just called them mahogany.

Then to make matters even worse they invented their veneer making method of peeling the log with a device copied from an old-fashioned apple peeler. This gave them gigantic sheets of veneer resulting in minimum of waste, and also an even-grained, completely figureless veneer which they then proceeded to teach the American common man was the best because it was regular and didn't have any "flaws" of figuring in it. This resulted in a style of furniture designed only for easy machine manufacturing that is known as Early Chicago or Motel Nothing.

INLAY WOODS. From the earliest times of our historical era small quantities of particularly beautiful or unusual woods have been imported to Europe and America for use in decorative inlays. And you will also find that many pieces in inlays are a pure white wood such as holly, that has been stained, especially in leaves, for in-

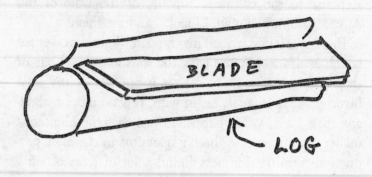

Method of peeling continuous sheet of veneer from a log of modern so-called mahogany which eliminates waste and results in an even figure of absolutely no interest. Both the blade and the log are about eight feet long, and the commonest example of the results is your standard four foot by eight foot piece of plywood. And now you will tell me that this gives plywood an interesting grain. And you've got me. Except that it doesn't work that way with the pulpy African and Philippine woods they pass off as mahogany these days.

stance, where the color shades from dark to light. All
these woods can now be bought from the two companies
I recommend in the back of this book. And you can
even get pre-assembled designs, border strips and even
chess boards. These are now all made in the damndest
way which is far too hard to describe in words, so somewhere around here there should be a drawing. The results of this process are too perfect to look antique, of
course, but it is easy enough to rough them up by scor-
ing the lines between the pieces of wood with some
sharp pointed piece of metal and then wiping some stain
into the cracks. The best way to do this is first on the
naked wood, and then again after the surface has been
coated with a thin sealer coat of varnish. Only then do
you wipe your stain into the cracks that you have
scratched between the pieces.

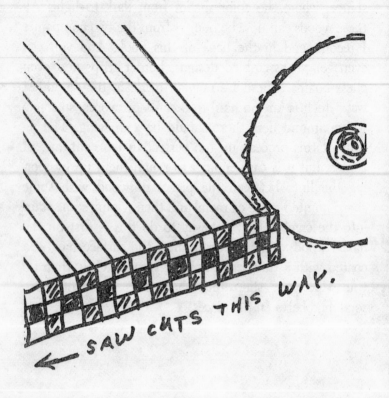

Method for mass-producing inlay strips. The block is glued-up of long strips of different colored woods, then sliced across the end. Assembling the block takes time and a lot of precise machinery, but it is still about a million times faster than hand work. This is why you can easily tell really old inlay work by the irregularities in the tiny hand-cut pieces.

2

Removing Old Finishes

I'd have to pull your leg pretty hard to convince you this part of refinishing is any "FUN"!

Wouldn't it be nice if you knew somebody who had a great big tank full of paint remover, big enough to put any piece of furniture in it? And he'd put your stuff in it over night. And the next morning pull it out and wash it clean with something that wouldn't soften the glue in the joints or even the glue holding on veneers. Wouldn't all that be nice?

Well, in these here modern times you can have it—even if you are going to have to pay that friend a few measly dollars. All you have to do is let your fingers do the walking for you through the "yellow pages" of your telephone directory. Because there are now thousands of places that do this kind of tank stripping and they are listed in the "yellow pages" under *Furniture Repairing & Refinishing*.

Of course if you're the kind of nut that has to do everything for himself, paint remover still comes in cans and I'm sure that you know where to buy it.

However, there may still be a few people around who don't know about my world-shaking discovery that most clear furniture finishes can be removed with a fifty-fifty mixture of lacquer thinner and denatured alcohol. And there are a lot of advantages of using this mixture. In the first place it is much cheaper than paint remover. Second, it is a much cleaner and easier job. Third, it won't burn your fingers or anything. And fourth, you don't need any drying time before applying a new stain or finish after using this mixture. (Both lacquer thinner and denatured alcohol are obtainable in any good paint and hardware store, and for real economy you can buy them in gallon cans.)

The way you use this magic formula is to pour roughly equal amounts of the denatured alcohol and lacquer thinner into a soup bowl—made of anything except plastic, which it will soften and sometimes dissolve right before your astounded eyes.

You then apply this freely to the condemned piece, working on a top or a side at a time, because it evaporates pretty fast.

You repeat this process until the finish is all soupy— the consistency that varnish would have when just brushed on. Now you can take the bulk of this off with any dull-edged blade. An old putty knife or a fried-egg

The only real secret of stripping is that old shellac and lacquer finishes will come off beautifully with a mixture of lacquer thinner and denatured alcohol, both available at your paint and hardware store. If your piece has paint on it, take it to a dipper-stripper. Look under "Furniture Stripping" in your Yellow Pages. That's supposed to be fairly rough steel wool in the soup bowl, and it's the best thing to use for wiping old finishes off with these solvents.

turner is ideal. Then you wash the remainder off and out of the corners with a piece of old toweling about as big as a washrag. (Or a washrag, of course.)

The technique for doing this is to alternately wipe off the surface and then rinse and squeeze out your rag in the bowl (kept full, of course) of our alcohol and lacquer thinner mixture. You can use your bare fingers for this process and you won't even notice it unless you have a cut which the alcohol will naturally sting but also keep mighty sterile. Your fingernails might get a little dirty, but that will go away in a few days. So if you are dainty, wear rubber gloves.

If you are now just going to apply a new finish, the surface will be ready in five minutes, which is a lot less time than it's going to take you to clean up the mess you've made. And I mean ready for any finish—from lacquer from a spray can to varnish with a brush.

However, if you plan to bleach or stain the wood, some residue of the old finish in the surface of the wood can make it hard for your bleach or stain to penetrate into the wood. In this case you must first scuff the surface with "o" or "oo" steel wool to allow for penetration. After doing this, you can also apply your bleach or stain with a pad of steel wool so that you can just rub a little harder anyplace where the stain or bleach is obviously not penetrating.

Now I don't want to get into any trouble with the sandpaper manufacturers, because sandpaper is good

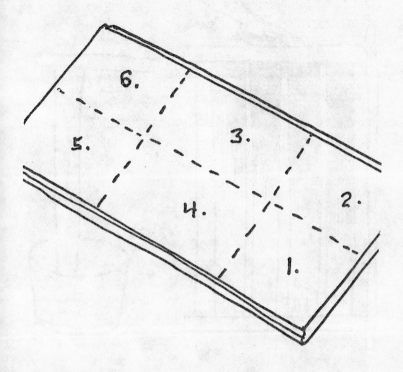

Try to make it easy for yourself when stripping. Don't just rush in and start slopping paint remover all over everything. First take anything apart that comes apart and work on a piece at a time. This is a table top with the leaves removed. And on big flat surfaces, work on one area at a time—especially when using lacquer thinner and/or alcohol. Take the time to do things neat—nobody is holding a stopwatch on you.

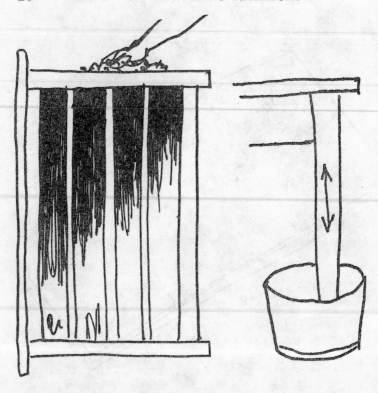

Here are two more ways to make it easier for yourself
when stripping. Put table legs in a small pan or old pot.
It saves the drippings, which you just keep brushing up
again. And for chests of drawers, keep rolling them
around so that you can work on the sides as if they were
tops.

It's the little things like this that make life more
bearable. And the trouble with your friendly local
stripper is that his chemicals fuzz your surface.

and useful stuff. In its place. Which is when you are making something from new wood. But in refinishing you almost never use it.

And the reason is this. Once you start with it, you are going to have to do every square inch of your piece with it because stain and bleach will not act the same on a freshly sanded surface as it will on the surface from which an old finish has been removed with rags or steel wool whether the vehicle was paint remover or my alcohol and lacquer thinner mixture.

Also for sandpaper to have any effect on an old finish you are going to have to start with at least medium, and then go down to fine and super-fine to remove the scratches of the rougher grades. Which is an incredible amount of work.

Naturally the same applies to using a scraper or small pieces of broken glass. Unless, of course, you are a French Canadian and you like the look of old pine that has been so scraped and then simply waxed. Which is alright with me. *Chacon a son gout,* as the old lady said as she kissed her cow.

3

Bleaching Out . . .

When necessary, when possible, and if you insist!

Two kinds of bleaches are used on wood. The first is to take the natural color out of wood. Mostly this is used for making "blonde" furniture, and so I've never used, and don't ever want to. But I've seen other people use it, and it works fine. It always comes in two bottles, and you just follow the directions. The big supply houses all sell it, and nowadays even some paint and hardware stores. Or they can order it if they really give a damn about you.

The other kind of bleach is the kind that takes the stain only out of wood. This is sodium hypochlorite, which is the only ingredient except water in all the liquid laundry bleaches such as Clorox.

You brush it on full strength. It isn't too hard on brushes except for bleaching some of them. But it will

Refinishing is really something of a seasonable sport—like gardening. There are some things that it is really best to wait until summer to do, because they take a lot of rinsing. This is especially true of bleaching and using lye to remove paint or to make an artificial antique. Lye will eat into the surface of wood to give it perfect "200-year-old patina." Will also turn most wood a terrific antique brown color.

chew up the hairs of really good ones. And it works right away if the Clorox is getting to the stain. A sealer in the wood could be preventing this, but this can be broken through with fine sandpaper.

As soon as the bleach has done its job, it should be rinsed off with water. When the wood is dry any trace of the bleach remaining in the wood can be neutralized by bathing it in vinegar then, after a minute or two, rinsing this off with water. Working with hard woods that are going to be stained the usual degree of dark this vinegar rinse is pretty superfluous. But if you have a porous wood on which you are going to put a pale stain, it is a good safeguard against pale streaks or the nerve-racking event of some stains freaking into pink or even mulberry as the residue of the bleach hits them about ten minutes after you have finished staining a piece.

Note: After bleaching softer woods or hard ones that are very old, it is sometimes necessary to fine sand the surface—or rub it with "ooo" steel wool—as the bleach tends to microscopically fray the fibres on the surface of the wood, which slightly obscures your ability to "see into" the grain or figures after the wood is finished. Of course, this may be exactly the look you are after as it is what some old woods look like. For more about all this, see the section on finishing.

4

Staining In . . .

In addition to color, you get the lovely illusion of depth.

Staining starts out with vegetable and animal dyes (squid) going back to ancient times, and I find that instant coffee is terrific. But the stains you buy in stores are products of modern chemistry. When they first came out in the early 1900's they were called analine dyes, and as some of them faded a lot in sunlight, that word analine got a bad name. So while that's what they still are—though now practically perfect—you don't see the word on the packages much. And if you do, don't be afraid of it anymore.

As these dyes are originally manufactured they come in powder form intended for mixing in either water, mineral spirits (same as turpentine), denatured alcohol or lacquer thinner. Such powders are still available in powder from the big suppliers I list in the back of the book, but mostly they come already dissolved in one of the four liquids.

Which is best? Without any shadow of doubt the ones dissolved in lacquer thinner (or sometimes it is a combination of lacquer thinner and denatured alcohol, but at any rate identifiable to you by the fact that they are always described as fast-drying).

The trouble with the water stains is that they raise the grain of the wood.

The trouble with "oil" stains (in a vehicle of turpentine, mineral spirits or varnish) is first that they take overnight to dry and aren't available in strong or dark shades or much variety of color.

The basic process of staining wood—whether it be a table top or tiny patch—is to brush the stain on freely and wipe it off with a dry rag while still damp or moist. This is so that your wood is colored only by stain that has sunk into it and not by any fine particles resting on the surface of the wood. This "loose" stain can get picked up and worked into streaks by any brushed on finish to come.

Of course the above doesn't apply if your stain is sprayed on by a regular spray gun (for furniture) or an air brush (for fine touch-up work). This is because when working with spray equipment you will also be spraying on your covering finish. (For more about spraying and how to do it see section on FINISHES later on in the section.)

Now we come to the heart of the matter in staining: the problem of getting an *exact* match. Exact as in *perfect*. Which certainly can be done. But here is one of the places we separate the men from the boys. And as my over-liberated wife always proofreads these pages, I hasten to add, also the girls from the women.

The problem is that you can't compromise about anything. For the sake of illustration, let's begin with a basic sort of problem. Let's say you have replaced a turned leg on a cherry table, and the problem naturally is to make it come out looking like the other three legs.

In the first place the new leg has got to be made of either cherry—or the one other possibility, WHITE POPLAR. The reasons cherry is in the first place are that you will have the same base color, grain and figure to start with that the fellow who stained the other three legs had. But how about white poplar?

White poplar is the great substitute wood for all restoration and fakery. The first reason, of course, is that it is almost white, so there is no underlying color to come out and fight your stain. The second is that it has an evenness of fibre size and hardness that makes it "take" stains perfectly. (White pine runs a poor second because it is too weak for legs, rungs, spokes, etc., and also because its lack of density means that any end grain showing will suck in stain like a blotter and turn that area much darker than the rest.)

Before we leave the subject, there is a slightly confus-

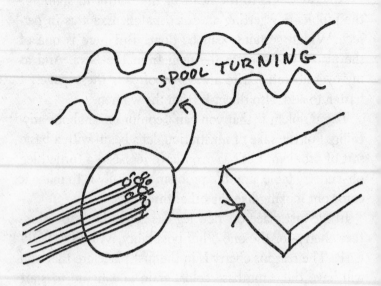

The problem of end-grain in staining is a natural result
of the tubular fibres of which wood is made. When
exposed in a board end or turning, these fibres suck in
more stain and get darker. The denser the wood, the less
problem, but it is always there to some extent. The
answer is to fill the end-grain before staining with
shellac. Brush the shellac freely on the turning then rub
off hard with rag dampened with denatured alcohol.
Then let the shellac that soaked quickly into the end
grain dry before applying stain. You may need two
coats—or thinner shellac—experimentation is necessary
to get the feel of this with different moods.

ing thing about white poplar, and that is that in plank form it has a very strong green streak running through the middle of it. And this can be pretty broad, too. But even with the green streak, it stains up to imitate cherry so well that it was used to make many fake cherry drop leaf tables from around 1840 to 1880. So never buy a cherry table without looking under it first for signs of this streak as such a table is worth a lot less than the real thing. Another way to tell the difference if the bottom of the top and leaves have been stained or painted is that poplar is a lot heavier than cherry.

Now the stain.

There is no question but that you are way ahead of the game if you use the fast-drying professional quality stains from one of the catalogue houses listed and discussed in the back of this book. Constantine or Craftsman have these stains, but I have to especially recommend Mohawk, because of the excellent color chart that they supply. And they have so many colors. So you can often find just what you need or at least start out very close, so that only a little tinting of the basic stain is necessary.

Naturally this means starting out with a set of stains that corresponds to an artist's pallet. The basic ones for tinting are the strong shades of:

RED MAHOGANY—for tinting things red, of course
MAPLE—for its high content of yellow
WALNUT—believe it or not for the blue in it

and these go into your basic wood colors: brown mahogany, brownish cherry, regular or palish walnut, the oaks, pines or whatever closest color you have selected from Mohawk's chart of about fifty different ones. (And in case you are involved with something exotic, they also have all the basic colors of the spectrum: red, orange, yellow, green, blue, indigo, violet. For memory fiends who want to never forget that list, the first letters of those colors can be thought of as spelling the name of my good friend "Roy G. Biv.")

The final stain mixing is done this way: you start with ten drops of your basic color and add one or two of the color in which direction you want your basic stain to move. To see what you've got, you try a brushfull (about three drops) of your mixture on a piece of the same kind of wood you are going to stain. So saving scraps of wood from the making of any replacement part is always a good thing, or you can test on the under-side of a table leaf, back of a leg or drawer-front, etc.

And so you just keep fooling around with your little drops of stain until you get to your correct proportion of colors as known in drops. Then you mix up a larger amount in that proportion.

A couple of more thoughts:

1. I am assuming that you realize that the color of the stain while still wet is the color it will be when a finish is applied to it.

2. In the name of Allah, I beg you—please don't try

to mix or tint a stain in a bunch of old screw caps from cans and bottles. This is such a messy way to live. Do it right. Go to an art supply store and get what they call a divided pallet—like the top of a tin water color box only with more separation or little bowls. Or a plain old muffin tin.

5

Finishes

For beauty and protection some easy ways and harder ones that are harder.

Well, I suppose the first question you have is why should I complicate your life by telling you about more than one finish. Why not just tell you the best and let it go at that? Well, the trouble is, some are easier to do than others, and the others (that are harder to do) are tougher than the ones that are easier to do.

The easiest one, which is shellac, is fine if you are just going to look at it. While varnish, which is the hardest, will stand up to wear, pretty hot plates and even alcohol —as in spilled booze or perfume. And in between these you have lacquer, which is a special case for several reasons, and a compromise between lacquer and varnish that modern furniture manufacturers have settled for. You may, too. I often do. But anyway, just so you get the whole picture let's take them up one at a time, and then look at some opaque finishes.

SHELLAC

We'll start out with shellac because it alone goes back a few hundred years, being the resin extruded from a tree in India when attacked, as I assume is commonplace, by some bug or other. This comes orange or bleached relatively clear (when it is ridiculously called "white," this being especially stupid as there is also a shellac with a lot of white pigment in it used as a primer, or first coat, in interior house painting, because it seals knots in wood that would bleed into regular paint).

Orange or clear shellac dissolves in and is thinned by —or even easily washed off with—denatured alcohol. It dries fast. You can get it from shiny to any degree of dullness by rubbing it with from fine to pretty rough pads of steel wool. Grades "oooo" (very fine) to "o" (pretty rough). Or you can easily raise its shine to a mirror gloss by rubbing it with a pad soaked in oil (any oil, though linseed oil is traditional) before it is completely dry. In fact when it has just become dry enough to touch lightly. This is the historic "French polish." (This result can also be achieved by rubbing liquid shellac onto a piece of wood with a pad soaked in oil—though the wood should first be primed with an initial brushed on coat of shellac. This way the glossy finish can be built up indefinitely.)

So then why has shellac fallen out of use? For lots of reasons. In a dry atmosphere it cracks. In a damp one it gets cloudy. Water on it turns it white in a few hours, and a strong martini will actually dissolve it so that a rag will wipe it off when you are cleaning up after all the drunks have gone home.

But it is still awfully easy to use because it sets up so fast—in a few minutes. And this means that if you have made any mistakes, you can wipe it off in a few minutes with cloths dipped in denatured alcohol and start all over again.

Lacquer is where modern chemistry has come from shellac to answer the needs of all kinds of finishers from factories to museums. Starting out as a kind of liquid celluloid in the early 1900's, it has now been perfected in many a marvelous breed for every purpose.

Different degree of dullness can be built into it. It can be made alcohol proof and won't blush, cloud, white spot or crack. It can be made with oils in it so that you can pad it on over a scuffed old finish to instantly resurface it. Or it can be combined with an amalgamator that makes it possible to brush it over an old cracked shellac finish (or an early bad lacquer one) to restore perfectly.

BRUSHING LACQUER

This kind of lacquer is relatively slow drying—about fifteen minutes—has excellent self-leveling qualities and goes on a lot thicker than shellac. As such, it is useful for fine touch-up work with a small camel's hair brush such as used for water colors. And in this way you will use it on almost every material discussed in this whoooole book.

And naturally brushing lacquer can be used on larger surfaces such as chests and table tops, but it isn't really good for this because brushing lacquer tends to pick up any stain in the wood which can result in light patches and streaks of the stain in the lacquer. The alternatives, of course, are spraying the lacquer on or brushing on varnish, which we will now go into.

SPRAYING LACQUER

The only point in using a spraying lacquer, which dries on the surface in seconds, is speed of production. You cannot only spray a piece in a fifth of the time it takes to brush coat it, but also your drying time is virtually eliminated. Five or ten minutes drying time is all you need between coats and fifteen minutes for your last coat. And between coats it rubs down with "ooo" or "oooo" steel wool beautifully and also a lot faster than you can rub a varnish.

The trouble is, you have to buy the machine and have a place to use it and then learn how to use a spray gun. So the only time an antiques restorer would use one is if he was running a full time refinishing shop. In such an event, instructions for use and cleaning come with the set-up. But in case you have one without instructions, the only trick involved is that you spray in cross strokes, starting near you and moving away so that over-spray doesn't settle on areas already sprayed. And by spraying in "strokes" I mean that you pull the trigger to start your cross-spraying movement and take it off the trigger at the end of each stroke.

For touch-up spraying you can, of course, use an air brush. And these are becoming very popular since you no longer need a compressor. They can now be operated by tanks of air that will spray a pint of fluid—which is an hour's worth of touching up—for around two dollars.

This concept of selling canned air has also led to a tremendous new development for professional furniture restorers: a portable lacquer finish sprayer with enough power to really work. (Previous ones didn't have enough pressure in the air can so that you had to thin your lacquer too much, or were driven by electric vibrators that didn't put out enough pressure either.) These are available from Mohawk—see catalogue listing in Appendix—and they are a marvel of simplicity and performance. Very easy to keep clean, too. See illustration for more details.

PADDING LACQUER

This lacquer is manufactured only by companies supplying professional refinishers. (See catalogue descriptions in back of book.) They are all secret and probably

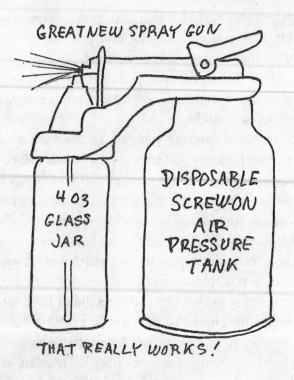

GREAT NEW SPRAY GUN

4 OZ GLASS JAR

DISPOSABLE SCREW-ON AIR PRESSURE TANK

THAT REALLY WORKS!

Each pressure tank will spray four jars of liquid thinned to the same consistency you would use with a regular compressor-run spray gun. The electric ones look good, but their vibrator mechanisms will only drive water-thin liquids.

You can get these from a terrific mail-order outfit called: Brookstone Company, Peterborough, N.H.—03258.

Just send them a card and ask for a catalogue. It's full of hard to find tools and things. Tell them I sent you.

patented formulas, but the result is a lacquer that you wipe on in a continuous motion with a pad of lint-free cloth (about ten layers thick and made from an old sheet or pillow case). This sets as you wipe it on with the same pressure you would use to polish wax, so the pad must always be lifted off the surface in motion or it will stick to the surface. It is not a hard trick to learn, and you just keep applying a little more lacquer to the cloth to gradually build up as thick a finish as you need.

This lacquer is very thin, so it is not used to start a finish. The wood must first have at least one sealer coat of shellac, lacquer or varnish already on it. What it is really incredibly good for is putting a new top surface on old worn and scuffed finishes because it squeegies into the surface roughness and produces an absolutely perfect glossy surface. This can be done to a dining table in about fifteen minutes. Then after another fifteen minutes of drying time, this surface can be "cut" down to the degree of dullness you want by using "ooo" steel wool in long grain-following strokes. Finally a wax or oil-base polish is applied. This is the way a professional seems to be able to "refinish" a whole bedroom set in three hours.

Naturally the surface to which this is done must be very clean, and it takes three steps to clean an old finish:

First: Rub hard with a wet washrag to remove any water-soluble dirt.

Second: Rub hard with a rag wet with mineral
           spirits to remove any fat, duck grease or
           traces of wax.

Third: Rub hard in grain-following strokes with
           "ooo" grade steel wool.

Fourth: Dust the surface a lot with a dry brush
           and a flannel cloth (alternately three
           or four times) .

Incidentally, your old-fogy local cabinetmaker will
knock padding lacquer, but that is why he is an old
foggy (foogy? fogy?) . Padding lacquer is what the big
boys in the New York City shops use. Not to mention
Rome and Paris where I have also traveled at great expense to make sure you get the absolutely right dope in
this book.

AMALGAMATOR

This amounts to lacquer thinner with some secret ingredients in to make it less volatile. As a result it can be
brushed on an alligatored or very cracked old shellac or
lacquer finish, and after a few minutes of letting it soak
into the old finish, it can be re-brushed into a just-like
new finish. (Pre-cleaning as for padding lacquer is, of
course, also necessary for this.)

The secret ingredients in this stuff are supposed to
keep such rebrushed finishes from cracking again, but in

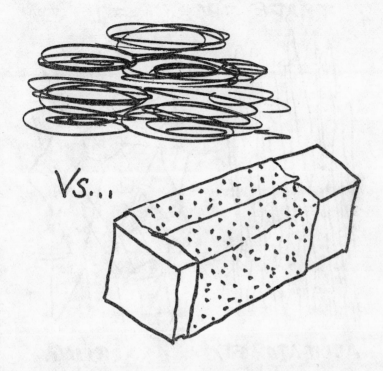

Vs...

That's ooo grade (fairly fine) steel wool on the left and fine garnet paper wrapped around a block of wood to keep it flat on the right. The steel wool is used to scuff the surface of a finish (shellac, lacquer or varnish) and will never cut through the finish to the wood to ruin all your hard work up to then. Like sandpaper will. Sandpaper is for smoothing wood—not finishes! So remember that, or you'll be sorry.

TRADE SECRET #1

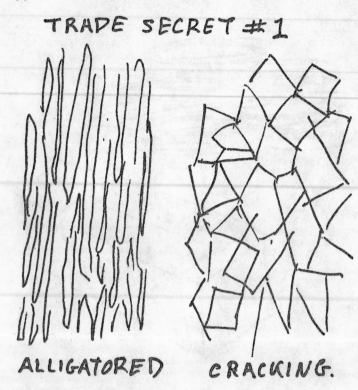

ALLIGATORED   CRACKING.

One of the niftier secrets of refinishing is that badly dried out old shellac finishes—and even ones that have turned white from exposure to damp air—can be made to look like new by brushing them with denatured alcohol (shellac solvent) or lacquer thinner. The finish simply re-dissolves in its solvent, and you just brush it smooth and let it dry. Then you buff it with steel wool just as you would a new finish and put a wax or polish on it.

case you have any doubts, a thin top coat of varnish will certainly make it stable.

This process is really only applicable to museum pieces in which you want to preserve the original stain under the finish that would be disturbed by removing the finish. Also the color of the old finish. But I just thought you would like to know about it anyway.

Modern professional varnishes—and even those at your local paint store—are a triumph of the chemical industry and in the last couple of decades have gotten as close to perfect as a product can get. The only thing you have to watch out for are the so-called "spar" varnishes because they are designed to dry on the surface but stay pliable underneath. This is fine for the masts of sailboats out in the extremes of weather all year. But this also makes it almost impossible to dull them with steel wool without the surface breaking and your steel wool getting caught in the gummy under part of the finish.

There are two troubles that people have with varnishing, but the cures for them are very simple.

The first is "fish-eyes," or open spaces that develop after you have finished applying a coat. This is because the surface wasn't cleaned and steelwooled before you started as fish-eyes are caused by non-adherence due to traces of wax or oil on the surface.

The second is dust specks, and what you have to understand here is that the dust is not going out of the air, and it is not because you didn't dust the surface well enough. They are going out of the brush if you have used it before. And I don't care how well you think you cleaned it if you then let it dry out.

So the solution of this problem is either to use a cheap new brush for every job, or to store your brush between uses of it by hanging it in its own private can of mineral spirits, the whole thing covered with a piece of aluminum foil and stored in its own private little cupboard.

And to keep your varnish clean, never dip your brush directly into the can, but pour some varnish out into a soup bowl, and dip your brush into that.

You can then apply the varnish as carefully as you want to, but I never have since I saw a couple of perpetually soused painters applying varnish to the transom of a yacht in a boatyard out in Greenport, Long Island one summer. They were putting it on in tough cross strokes as if they were trying to beat up the wood. When the whole surface had been covered this way—and fast, so they would have an extra five minutes to sit under the boat and have another drink before the foreman came by again—they just tipped it off, and it dried perfectly.

Their point in the hard brushing was to get a thin coat to prevent sagging on the vertical surface and to prevent "skips" (small uncovered areas). So ever since I've been varnishing the same way. And since I use small cans of fresh varnish and a cheap new brush for each job, varnishing is easy.

As a matter of taste you can, if you want, thin your varnish slightly for easier brushing. You need only about a tablespoonfull of mineral spirits to a cup.

THE GREAT MYTH ABOUT VARNISH & DUST

Every time I give a lecture some poor soul in the audience asks me how I get rid of the "invisible" dust in the air that causes "specs" in his varnish. Well the truth is that there isn't any such dust. If you can't see it it isn't there. And if it was heavy enough to fall on your table top, it would have fallen to the floor before you started. Nope, the trouble is he's got a dirty brush, even though he'll never believe me.

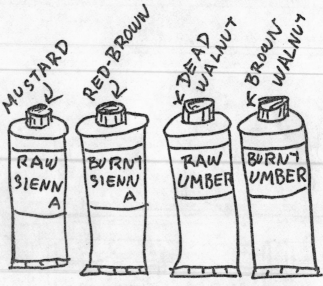

THE BASIC "EARTH" COLORS

Regular furniture stains are clear, like wines or colored glass. That is because they are dyes, with no pigment in them. But in every paint store you can buy tubes of heavily pigmented stains used for coloring paint that are generically called "colors ground in oil." And these are opaque enough that by wiping or smudging them on a surface you can conceal flaws in the wood or even make a poplar table look like a cherry one. By mixing the four colors above you can get any of the colors antique wood normally comes in. For some cherry tones you might want a little orange, too.

Lacquers, being as good as they are these days, the only time a professional finisher uses varnish is when he needs a top surface that will be subject to a lot of abuse, because while modern lacquers may be very good, modern varnishes are fantastic in resisting even such horrors as spilled perfume on a lady's dresser, pure straight gin soaking all night on a cocktail table and a flower pot with a hole in its bottom standing for a week with water seeping down out of it.

And even in such cases the common practice is to build up your finish of lacquer first, and then just one thin coat of varnish to top it off, because it is the nature of the varnish, not its thickness that does the job, and additional coats are a waste of time.

Patina is one of those words that is used a lot by smarter-than-thou know-it-alls who don't know what they are talking about. They tell you in their invariably smug manner that a true patina can only be obtained by aging or use of years of hand polishing.

Well, a patina—on a finish—is plain and simply the scuffing and marks of wear. And it would be an unimaginative refinisher who couldn't easily duplicate them with a hard rubbing of steel wool (grade "ooo"), some scratches with rough steel wool (grade "1"), some judicious use of loose fine sand and a little garnet paper here and there where wear would likely be stronger—and in one or two unlikely places for wear which is the master touch in all fine lying. Then you finally wax the piece

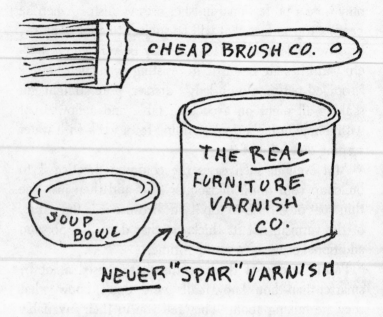

NEUER "SPAR" VARNISH

You want an alcohol-proof table top? Just lay one thin coat of varnish over the present finish. And the secret to a trouble-free job is that you buy a cheap new brush and a small fresh can of varnish for every job. And then you add 5% to 10% mineral spirits (paint thinner) to the varnish to make it spread nice and thin. You do that in the bowl. And be sure you get a varnish specifically recommended for furniture on the label. Avoid "spar" varnish as you would cholera—it will never get really dry.

sparingly. An oil-base polish would make your patina less visible.

A second kind of patina is the kind that occurs on the surface of unfinished wood that has been sitting around in the air for a hundred or more years. Through the effect of alternately damp and dry days and seasons the fibres on the surface of the wood become loosened to form a microscopic fuzz on the surface of the wood. Then someone comes along and waxes or shellacs the surface (you see this most often in primitive or country-built chairs), and although matted down now the fibres still impart a vague obscurity to the surface of the wood.

The duplication of this look is also no problem for your restorer who wants to duplicate this look on, say, the leg of an Early American Windsor chair on which he has just replaced a leg.

The new raw leg is simply bathed in a lye solution (a full can of crystals sprinkled gradually into a quart of water). This will loosen the fibres on the surface of the wood, but also turn it dark brown. After rinsing the leg in cold water, this brown stain disappears immediately when the leg is soaked with Clorox. Then rinse well in hot water, dry thoroughly and wax or finish.

I have a couple of pieces in my living room to which just for the fun of it I have done this. Both are reproductions made around 1930, but I now pass them off as "oh, around two hundred years old." So far only one person has laughed at me out of over a hundred I've shown the pieces to. And he is one of those honest old Yankees that was doing the same thing before I was born. And at that, what he caught me on was a design detail that was wrong, which I could have corrected in the beginning if I had understood it.

ANTIQUED OPAQUE

The idea of applying a transparent glaze onto a colored surface goes back as far as Ancient Greece in our western line of civilization—as well as from the beginnings of Eastern and Oriental cultures. The basic purpose of this practice is to accentuate or give more depth to carved or irregular surfaces. And then it has been used secondarily to make things look older by simulating the grime and dirt that collect in the crevices of old and well used pieces. Thus we have the common use of the word "antiqued" when what we really mean is glazed.

All kinds of materials can be used as a base coat and a glaze and they can both be many colors for a wide variety of effects. The commonest example in our world of antiques is the "antique white" French chair of the Louis' and even earlier Italian furniture. After all, if the French could steal their cuisine from northern Italy, why not their furniture, too?

In a classic ancient piece the whole chair would be smothered by rubbing plaster into the surface of the wood. Then it was all gold leafed and burnished. Over this would be applied a white shellac of lacquer, and finally the glaze would be brushed on and wiped off the protruding surfaces of the carving. And then a little more hard rubbing on the wear points would allow the gold to peep through.

Such an effect has been mass-produced for years with the addition of fine spatterings of black paint as a sort of stylized worm-hole and a random chipping of white lacquer, both of which practices come under the term distressing.

As such finishes are supposed to have more charm the more beat-up they look, the only restoration that would be appropriate would be touching them up with lacquer and glaze. Or with white shellac sticks and glaze.

CHINESE LACQUER

Mostly found on boxes and trays, but sometimes on furniture, the originals were brought back from the Orient by sailing ships as soon as the British Empire began trading around the world. The base material is now sold as Japan Colors, which is a heavily pigmented lacquer "paint." The finish now, as then, is applied by brushing on a number of coats and sanding each smooth with very fine garnet paper. The final glossy effect is achieved by padding on the last coat and even a coat of clear lacquer over that if desired. The old term for this was "French polishing." Now we call it "padding" as in the entry above on PADDING LACQUER.

MILK PAINT

Unlike the preceding four novelty finishes which do not inherently relate to wood, milk paint was almost always used on it. And with obscure exceptions, milk paint is found almost exclusively on primitive Early American furniture. Because it was the only paint they had to cover up what they considered to be plain ordinary pine.

The term milk paint is a half misnomer, because it was made by mixing milk with buckets of blood collected at slaughtering time, offering a range of colors from pale pink to dark red, depending on the proportions used. But also strong colored clays were locally mixed with milk, and to a limited extent (because of its cost) yellow and blue pigments imported from England.

This paint was used on virtually all Windsor chairs as again the wood just wasn't considered to be worth looking at since it wasn't figured like mahogany and walnut. So even today the scraped-down Windsor chair is not for you purists, even traces of the original paint left on the scraped-down ones are considered a plus value.

On blanket chests this paint was also given a crude but very attractive false graining by swirling around some darker colored paint on the base surface before it was dry. Often with a date in the middle. And this effect can easily be reproduced even by your tyro forger. It can be done with ordinary oil-base paints, your flat latex paints or you can even make up some milk paint using powdered milk and powdered dry color. Then, of course, you will want to batter the piece around with a chain and then give it a couple of coats of dirty shellac.

6

Patching & Concealing

The deceptive arts of visual obsfucation and illusion.

Of all the tricks in an antique restorer's bag, none is more important than the combined use of shellac or lacquer sticks and touch-up powders. For not only do they permit you to work miracles of visual deception on wood, but also on stone, ceramics, metal, glass—anything rigid.

But their use is nowhere near as widespread as it should be because people are afraid of them. They think that they are too hard to use, and this belief is encouraged by professional restorers, who are an ancient craft guild type. To scare people off they even go so far as to call the sticks "burn-in" sticks and the process of using them "burning-in." And the whole thing isn't anything like that. There is no burning, with all its dangerous connotations, at all. The sticks are *melted* at a very low, safe heat such a low heat in fact that they will not hurt any finish at their hottest.

① FIRST THE SCRAPED HOLE IS CLEAN

② PATCHING STICK "SHELLAC" IS MELTED AND DRIPPED INTO HOLE

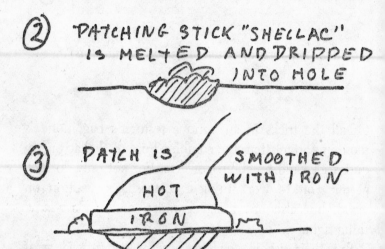

③ PATCH IS SMOOTHED WITH IRON

HOT IRON

④ EMERY CLOTH WRAPPED AROUND FELT BLOCK IS USED FOR SMOOTHING.

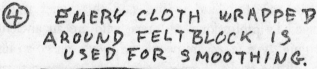

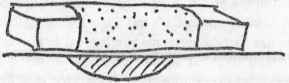

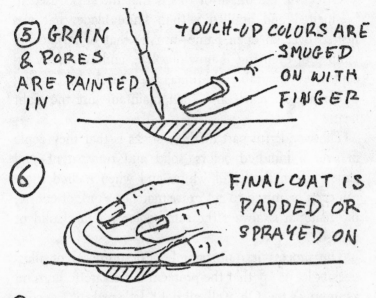

⑤ GRAIN & PORES ARE PAINTED IN

TOUCH-UP COLORS ARE SMUGED ON WITH FINGER

⑥ FINAL COAT IS PADDED OR SPRAYED ON

⑦ BUFFED WITH "0000" STEEL WOOL + WAXED OR POLISHED

I don't really believe that you could learn to use patching or "burn-in" sticks from this, but it does give you an idea of what you are up against. I don't think anybody could learn it without watching it be done by somebody who already knows how. You just have to watch him once for a half an hour. The rest is practice on your own. You find such people to watch in the back rooms of furniture stores, buzy as bees.

Of course the origin of this is that the sticks used to be melted and applied with a knife blade that was heated over an open flame—usually that of an alcohol lamp. But even this is now obsolete, and everybody except a few incurable old-timers uses an electric ironing tool made to reach and then maintain just the right heat.

The wonderful part of these sticks is that they come in over a hundred colors, solid and transparent—and about fifteen shades of white—and when melted these can even be mixed to get *exact* matches. And, of course, the material is always the same color whether solid or melted.

The process is quite simple. For purposes of illustration, let us say that the problem is a cigarette burn on a mummy's toe, Oh, well, all right, let's make it the edge of the top of a Louis XIV side table.

First you scrape the charred wood out with the blade of a sharp penknife, getting all the black away from the edges, but leaving perhaps some in the center of the bottom of the crater you are digging.

If the wood in your hole shows up a lot lighter than the rest of the table top you can stain it to a pretty close match with a quick drying liquid stain. Or you can smudge in some touch-up powder. (Which we will get to in the next section.)

Now you drip into the hole a mixture of your sticks that as a beginner you will have melted together in a teaspoon held over an alcohol lamp. Later on you can do this right on your iron. With the iron you now press this glob smooth with the surface of the table top and finally sand off any extra with some very fine garnet paper wrapped around a perfectly flat block of hard felt.

With padding lacquer (see above) you smooth the area, conceal any signs of your patch by smudging tiny bits of touch-up powder over them, polish them in with some more padding lacquer, and then go over the whole top with padding lacquer so it will all have the same degree of shine to it. Which you can then dull with steel wool if desired.

Simple, isn't it?

Now about those touch-up powders I just mentioned.

TOUCH-UP STAINS

Like the shellac sticks these powder stains come in a wide range of colors. They also have the fine quality of not changing color or shade whether wet or dry or mixed into padding lacquer—or any lacquer or even shellac, for that matter. This makes them the ultimate material for the antiques restorer—or forger, too, of course. And like the heat sticks they can also be used on many other materials besides wood.

So where do you get these magic powders? Again I must recommend Mohawk as the best source because of their giant color chart. And you can order them from the Mohawk catalogue either individually or in their intelligently selected sets.

7

Repairing

The hard part is to learn how to think about repairing.
Then you've got it licked!

Well, I don't want to go very far with this, because there
are many, many good books already available on this
subject. Not to mention a steady flow of articles in the
magazines. So I think I should only refer to the aspects
of woodworking that specifically apply to antiques, and
these you will find in the second part of this chapter that
takes up specific problems commonly encountered.

So in the next few pages I will limit myself to giving
some reckless advice to anyone who wants to set up a
shop for repairing antiques as opposed to making furniture and so on from raw wood. And the difference between the two kinds of shops lies in the nature of the
tools you will use more often in repairing than in building.

The hand tools are about the same in both cases, except that the repairer will be using chisels and files and woods rasps more often. The repairer will also have much more need for a large vice that can be well padded with layers of woolen blanket or felt to hold finished pieces of wood—like the carved leg of a Chippendale chair while you are trying to put on a new foot.

Also you will run across gluing jobs that will take about a dozen various sized C-clamps with pieces of soft pine or hard felt glued to their pressure-exerting surfaces.

For knocking loose jointed chairs and other things apart, you will also need a mallet whose head is made of rolled felt or leather. Or at least an ordinary hammer whose head has been softened by wrapping many layers of pieces of woolen blanket around it.

And speaking of gluing, which is what ninety-five per-cent of all repair work on wood consists of, the ubiqui-tous white glues are fine for regluing fairly tight joints and for tacking small pieces onto larger pieces where there is no strain in use. But for serious gluing there is no substitute for good old Weldwood plastic resin powder. The wood around it always breaks before this glue will. And if you mix it with sawdust to make a paste in stuffing loose joints you will never go wrong, because it hardens without shrinking like cast iron.

On the negative side forget all about the syrupy brown glues. One of these has a famous name and you see it everywhere, but there ought to be a law against selling it. Which also goes for the brown flake glues that

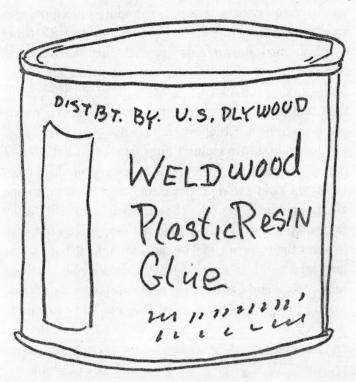

Never let it be said that I criticized the modern white glues that are on the market under a hundred trade names these days. But they can soften under sustained moist conditions. Even so, they are fine for tight fitting joints where moisture will never get. But Weldwood not only penetrates wood fibres, but turns into some kind of rock. The only reason for not using it all the time is that you have to mix up little batches each time by adding water to the powder.

you have to heat up in a pot, fish glue, hide glue, etc. and the brown syrup division. The trouble with these old fashioned brown glues is that they are not waterproof or even slightly resistant to moisture after they have dried. Thus moist weather will loosen them, and they account for all the antique tables, chairs, chests and everything else that ever fell apart.

Personally, I love gluing things together. That's how I got in trouble with Steve Cook's eleven-year-old daughter. The Cooks live right down the street from us, so one afternoon when I found a chair in their house that really fascinated me with its ricketiness, I just walked out with it when they weren't looking and brought it back a few days later solid as a rock with Weldwood. So that evening Steven and Gertie (that's his wife) were wondering aloud at the dinner table what they could do for me to pay back the favor.

That's when their eleven-year-old daughter piped up with, "Well, if he gets such a kick out of gluing old chairs, why not just give him another one to glue!" (Nope, I don't make these things up. They really happen.)

And finally, another negative word about these contact glues that are like a thick, tan rubber cement, which have been especially pushed for attaching veneers. They seemed great when they first came out, but the passage of time has revealed that in some cases for some unknown reason they begin to loosen.

OLD LEG

A NEW PIECE IS BEST HELD ON WITH DOWEL

Of course, the best way to reattach or replace a piece of leg is with a dowel and Weldwood. No iron screws or straps will ever work. They will always loosen, but a glued dowel won't. What the above drawing doesn't explain is how you hold your extension on the old leg while you drill your hole through it. Well, the answer is that you flattened both joint surfaces and glued your extension "foot" on to the leg the day before. Just so it would stay in place for the drilling operation. But it is the dowel glued in that really does the job.

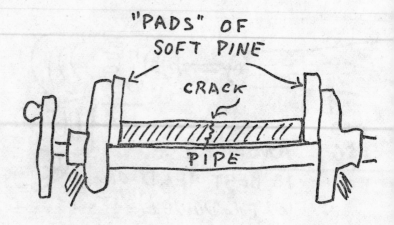

PIPE CLAMPS. *The head and foot fit onto a ¾" pipe of any length so that you can clamp wide or long things. Shown here is just a table leaf, but you can even use them to hold a seven-foot long sideboard together while your glue dries in its joints. The two pieces of the clamp come off the pipe easily, so you usually just leave them on a five foot length of pipe, keeping shorter and longer lengths of pipe in reserve.*

The pads are a must, as these clamps exert a tremendous pressure. Of at least three-quarter inch pine, the pads should extend three inches on each side of the clamp.

In power tools the big difference is that the repairer will prefer a small band saw to a table saw. This is obviously because in antiques you have a lot more curved lines than straight ones. But, of course, it's still nice to have both.

And you'll be a lot happier if you have two quarter-inch drills, one with a bit in it for sinking dowels and the other with a disc sander on it. It's just that it's a lot handier to have them both lying around ready for use.

Incidentally, in repairing antiques you will be using a lot more dowels than screws. They are easiest to sink tightly and are more permanent because they have the same coefficient of expansion as the wood around them. Also your glue can bond into them as it can't screws. In fact the only use for screws in any cabinet work is to hold two flat pieces tightly glued together while the glue dries.

And as far as the obscenity of screwing iron angles and straps onto furniture goes, I can't even think about that without getting nauseous. It isn't enough that they look terrible, but they don't work. Again the problem is the different coefficient of expansion. Your wood may be expanding in the heat of summer and shrinking in winter only a minute amount, but that damn iron is shrinking and expanding a lot less—with the result that any such repair is bound to tear itself apart in time.

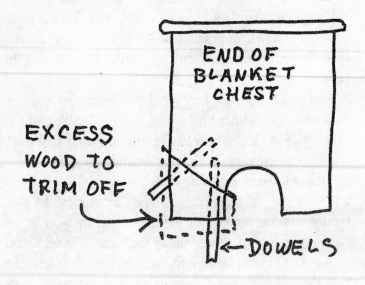

BASIC METHOD OF PATCHING "BOARD." *Let's say the above is the end of a blanket chest with one leg smashed off and lost. First you establish a straight flat edge on the leg by running it through a table saw. (Having taken the end off the chest first, of course.) Then you rough out a new leg a little oversize and give it a matching straight flat edge on the saw. This gives you a joint that will stay glued.*

In some cases you may want to add a ¼" dowel as shown or glue a reinforcing strip inside the leg. Near the edge so your "C" clamps can reach it. No screws or nails, please.

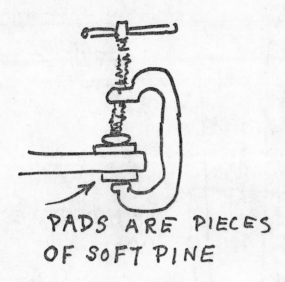

PADS ARE PIECES
OF SOFT PINE

"C" CLAMP. *This could be an illustration of how two of these would be used to reinforce that new foot on that blanket chest in another illustration somewhere around here. But it isn't, because there is no second piece of wood being held to the one piece in the drawing. Which makes this a pretty silly drawing, except to show what a "C" clamp looks like and that their clamping faces have to be padded so they don't chew into the wood being clamped. (Well, if you must know, the truth is that by the time it came to write this caption it was too late to correct this stupid drawing!)*

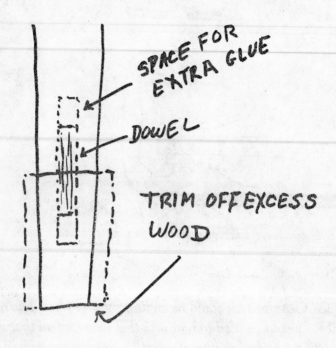

SPACE FOR EXTRA GLUE

DOWEL

TRIM OFF EXCESS WOOD

Basic method of patching leg. *As with board, you first get yourself two flat surfaces. Then you drill into both of them to receive a short piece of dowel. By making your added piece oversize as shown above you don't have to worry about not having your dowel holes exactly matching. After the joint is dry, you simply trim off the excess wood on the new piece.*

It is really a shame that they still allow the old hide and
hoof glues to be sold. And that includes any brown
liquid glue of the mucilage family. They are all right for
package-sealing tape, but in furniture any exposure to
moist air will soften them, and in a few years give you a
loose joint. But the new white glues such as Elmer's
won't do this, and for super-super strength there is
nothing like good old Weldwood Plastic Resin Glue.

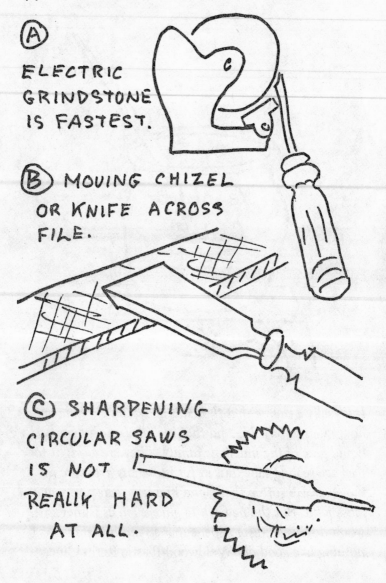

(A) ELECTRIC GRINDSTONE IS FASTEST.

(B) MOVING CHIZEL OR KNIFE ACROSS FILE.

(C) SHARPENING CIRCULAR SAWS IS NOT REALLY HARD AT ALL.

SHARPENING

Trying to sharpen blades and other edges with carbo-rundum stones is something else that drives me up a wall. My Uncle Jake used to be able to do it, but time never meant anything to him anyway. So I was delighted when I got a job in a furniture action factory and one of the old timers there showed me you could get just as fine an edge on a motor driven grindstone if you were careful not to let the steel get too hot as this burns the fine edge right off. Just don't press very hard and keep cooling the blade in water or oil.

And an even more practical way to keep a chisel blade sharp is by pulling it *across* a file. This is also how you resharpen a circular saw three or four times before it needs a professional job because you eventually foul up the "set," which is the alternate slanting of the teeth to left and right.

8

Carving

The whole trick is to multiply your expectation of how long it will take by about ten.

The first thing about carving is that it is only sensible with certain "good-carving" woods. White pine sounds good because it is so soft. But it is so weak that it will chip out. That is to say, pieces will break off accidentally at the slightest wrong pressure. Also a blade tends to slip on it and not cut in exactly as directed.

The ideal wood for carving is Honduras mahogany, and second best are the heavier, denser African and Philippine imitation mahoganies. A little harder but with just as much response to the blade is American cherry. Then come the walnuts because they have a slight tendency to splinter as you cut them. Not much, but a little.

The way you use the blade—like good driving—is defensive. Your objective is to cut away slices and wedges of wood without splintering it or busting out pieces you don't want to. And attacked brutally enough even the best carving woods can be made to splinter and break.

Of course, carving tools are useful, or they wouldn't exist. But I've never seen a job of carving that couldn't, with a little bit of patience, be done with the small blade of a very sharp penknife. Or do I mean the very sharp blade of a small penknife? And that's a good way to start to get the feel of carving. Then real carving tools will be a delight because you can work about five times faster.

About that sharp blade. This is where it is all at. And so some people resort to Exacto knives, but the trouble with them is that you can't hold them close enough to the point as you can with a penknife, a carving tool or a thin chisel (which is in essence a straight-blade carving tool). The point being that you get to push the blade away from you.

So sharpening is the problem, and the first point is that some steels sharpen better than others, and the basic thing you have to watch out for is stainless steel. I don't know why, but it just doesn't sharpen well. As to sharpening a cutting edge, you can use a file, a stone or revolving stone, and you can find that in the section on *Repairs*.

I was going to start out by saying that about the only thing you can't do with wood is cast it. But then I remembered that you can. The medallions and bas-relief decorations you see on cabinet doors and panels is a wood pulp cast in molds. And, of course, you can do the same thing for some repairs by mixing sawdust with glue and modeling it with a greasy blade or pressing it with wax paper. When this is fine-sanded after drying, this will take stain. Use a white glue. Weldwood is too hard to take any stain. Then with touch-up powders you can make the surface indistinguishable from the real thing.

Part II

How to Do It from A to Z

Being an alphabetical approach to the specific problems you will run into, plus a few you'd love to have.

ARMOIRES

This is the French word for what the English call a clothes press and Americans are at a loss to call anything except to describe it as a free-standing closet or cupboard for hanging up your clothes. But there is a very good reason for using the French word, and that is that the ones you find in the United States are coming down (by the truck-load) from Canada's French speaking (and acting) province of Quebec.

They are about five to six feet tall and have two full length doors on the top. Some are empty inside, others have had shelves put in. Structurally they are of floating panel construction. That is to say that the sides and doors are made of wide boards fitted into slotted frames. And as they are of "primitive" construction this is plainly obvious.

Usually they were painted—originally—lovely pale blues and yellows with milk-base paint. Whenever found with such original paint it should be preserved at all costs, and badly worn or scuffed areas should be touched up a matching color. This can be done with any flat water paint such as the poster paints that come in jars or flat interior wall paints that dilute with water. Several major paint companies supply a wide variety of tinting colors which you can add to white to get any color and shade you want.

Should you ever want to remove any of the original

paint—say, because there isn't enough left to be worth saving—straight ammonia will do it best. Should the ammonia darken the wood, it can be returned to its natural color (after the ammonia has dried thoroughly) by flushing it with Clorox.

Sophisticated French Canadians value these pieces especially as their panels have been carved to show a raised diamond shape in each panel. Then they simply scrape the wood with pieces of broken glass and wax it well. They just don't seem to care about the original paint the way us American connoisseurs do.

If you want to buy a couple of thousand of these, I suggest you go to the vast antique storage barns of Rene Beaudoin in the small town of Defoy in the Province of Quebec. This town lies about a half mile south of the super highway that connects Montreal and the city of Quebec. Leaving Montreal it is about three-fifths of the way toward Quebec, but you will have to get a Canadian road map to find it, as it is not shown on U.S. maps that show that southern part of Canada.

Of course, I'm pretty snobby about preserving old original paint, but I don't suppose anyone will shoot if you stain and varnish one of these. Or even paint it and decorate it peasant style. In fact, I saw one in Boston not long ago that had been painted pure vermillion, stripped with gold and then wiped with a dark brown antique glaze. Which is about as far as you can go, but I'll have to admit that it was stunning if you go in for that sort of dramatic effect.

BEDS

The characteristic trouble with old beds is that the people who made them didn't have sense enough to make them in sizes that fit modern springs—inner or otherwise. The big problem, of course is that they are all too short, because people used to be shorter.

The solution to this is shown in our accompanying illustration—as well as how headboards are made to fit in a slightly wider frame.

Since these stretchers are usually made of a very hard and well-seasoned wood, this is not a job for an amateur carpenter, so after taking your measurements you are going to have to take your stretchers to someone who has some heavy-duty saws and experience in using them. You need straight cuts so the glue can bind the pieces together under the pressure of clamps. *Weldwood*, of course, is an excellent glue to use for this. Another effective method would be to drill holes and fit them with steel bolts, although it is a lot more trouble and not really necessary.

Naturally your "new wood" patching piece is made a little oversize so you can trim it down and then stain to match.

I'll admit I'm at a loss as to what else to say about

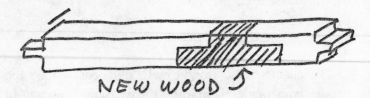

LENGTHENING AN OLD BED

NEW WOOD

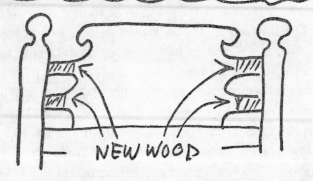

AND WIDENING A HEADBOARD

NEW WOOD

In both cases, you'll need a good table saw.

You really need heavy duty power tools to do a good job with this sort of thing. The stretchers are usually maple that has hardened with drying to the consistency of cast iron. But it is being done every day in places such as Leonard's Antiques on route 44 in Seekonk, Mass.— The world's greatest antique bed restorer's.

beds. Their being so big, you'd think there would be more. But obviously they are easy to refinish if you take them apart and work on the head and footboards as if they were table tops. And who ever heard of anybody breaking the leg off a bed?

BELLOWS

When one of the wooden pieces of a bellows has been broken we have a more interesting problem than is obvious at first glance. The broken off piece is almost certainly there, because it is attached to the leather. The problem comes when you try to clamp it in position while your glue dries. If you use only one clamp across the center, the ends of the piece won't be tight enough to make an invisible joining. And your diagonally placed clamps will slip off and/or cause the glued-on piece to slide in one direction or the other.

The solution to such a problem on any flat piece of wood is to place it on a wide board or rough table top and exert the clamping pressure between nails driven into the table. These are placed about a quarter of an inch from the edge of the bellows side, and then soft wooden wedges are driven or tapped in to establish the desired pressure.

This technique naturally applies to many other curvey pieces of wood such as chair backs where it may even be

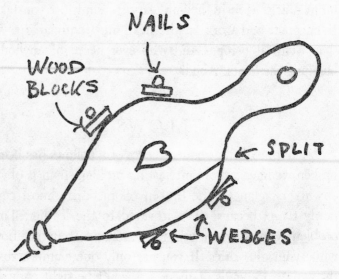

NAILS

WOOD
BLOCKS

← SPLIT

WEDGES

It's a bellows

This isn't all floating in space. The bellows is laid on a
board, the nails are driven into the board around it, then
the wood blocks and wedges are pushed in to exert
pressure while the glue hardens in the split. It is really
amazing how the curviest things can be repaired if you
have the patience to figure out or even custom-build a jig
to hold them together in. And the trick with multiple
breaks is not to try to do it all at once, but glue on a
piece a day. And that is the essence of patience.

worth your while to take the chair apart to be able to get your piece flat on a "nailing board."

Replacing the leather part of an old bellows is a job that doesn't take any particular skill or fancy tools. Finding the new leather is probably the hardest part, all this takes is a trip to your Yellow Pages to find the local company that repairs leather handbags, luggage and jackets. What they can't give you as scrap they'll sell you or tell you where to get it.

The first step is to clean off the edges of the wooden pieces. If the old leather can be taken off reasonably intact, you then use this as a pattern for your new piece. If not, use some old sheeting to establish a pattern by cutting a piece to approximate size and attaching it temporarily to the wooden pieces with rubber cement. Trim this getting the exact shape you need, then pull it off and use it as a pattern for cutting your leather.

The best glue to use (making sure you've first rubbed off the old rubber cement if you used it) is a white wood glue such as the ubiquitous *Elmer's*. And the tacks to use are the same kind upholsterers use, which are available in really big hardware stores, and certainly from upholsterers.

The trick in the actual process is not to try to glue the whole thing first, but to position the leather with a tack about every six inches. Then you glue and tack about four inches along at a time.

BLANKET CHESTS

Whether of the long, low variety or the "standup" kind with one or more drawers (real or fake), these invariably come in the rough with one or both hinges of the lift-top broken off and the wood under the hinges split from previous repairs attempted by some Visigoth using a sledge hammer or a pickaxe.

If the strap hinges need to be replaced, reproductions can be had from Old Guilford Forge, Guilford, Connecticut, ground to matching shape and antiqued. The "wire" type hinges from Horton Brasses, Berlin, Connecticut.

But that is only the beginning of the problem, because careful examination of the piece will reveal that the reason the hinges tore out or split the wood of the backboard wasn't just rough handling by some crude early settler. The real trouble was that over the years the board the top was made of has shrunk and is now anywhere from a quarter of an inch to an inch narrower. And when the front lip of the top is pushed down over the front of the chest, it has pulled on the screws holding the bottom half of the hinge to the back of the chest.

Obviously an adjustment is necessary. The hard way is to bend the lower half of your hinge so that the joint ex-

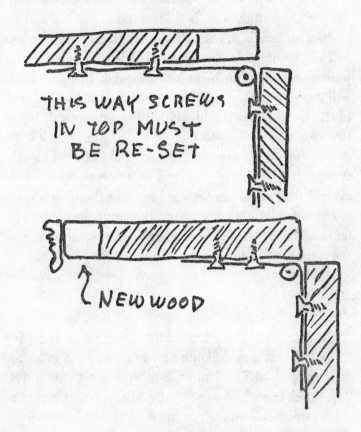

THIS WAY SCREWS
IN TOP MUST
BE RE-SET

NEW WOOD

The tops of old pine blanket chests usually contract over the years causing them not to close properly and/or tear their hinges off. The answer is to widen the top with a new strip of pine along the back edge, or along the front edge in back of the moulding.

tends forward far enough to take up the distance lost by the shrinkage of the top. See illustration.

Another way is to reset the screws that attach the top half of the hinge to the top of the chest. Though some purists will object to this on the grounds that the move will show due to the exposed screw hole and the paleness of the wood under the hinge that is now exposed. In either case a strip of wood may be added to the back edge of the top to restore it to its original width. Properly stained and distressed, this will never be noticed. Especially if the joint is camouflaged with touch-up powders.

Another alternative is to pry the front lip of the top off, and insert your widening strip between the lip and the front edge of the top.

BENTWOOD

This term usually refers to the furniture of the Victorian era that is now being exactly reproduced in Spain and shipped to the United States in great quantities. The problem with it is, of course, that when it breaks it splits and the wood springs apart so that it is very hard to clamp the wood together while the glue sets when you try to repair it. The solution to this problem is to have the patience to fashion hollowed-out blocks of wood to be used inside of your clamps. And you can also give the hollows in these blocks a non-slip surface by coating them with contact cement and letting it dry well. It is simply a matter of fooling around until you have good control of your clamping operation. (See also *Windsor Chairs*.)

BOWLS

The obvious way to refinish a wooden bowl—if you want to use it to mix salads—is to soak it with olive oil. The trouble with this, as with so many obvious things, is that it's wrong. The bowl may look all right, but you have to spend the rest of your life eating salads flavored with rancid olive oil. A far better finish for a bowl that is to be used is a penetrating wood sealer. Keep brushing it on for an hour until no more will sink in, then wipe off hard, and let dry a week. This will give you a surface as hard and tasteless as a plastic dish, and you can really scour it clean of all that nasty-smelling olive oil between salads.

Cracks are harder. Gluing won't work, because after a few months or a year a new crack will begin to appear just to one side or the other of your glued joint. But a glued quarter-inch dowel will work on one of the long bowls with handles on the ends. See illustration.

In the really hard case of the round bowl the only thing that will work is a butterfly patch, and this has the great advantage of looking antique itself as you often find old bowls mended this very way long ago. So such a

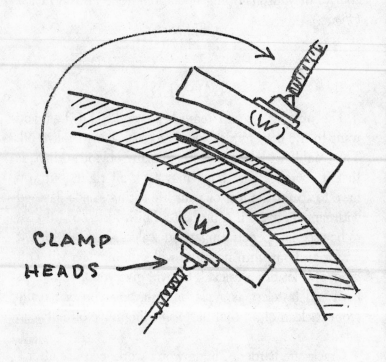

CLAMP
HEADS →

*Method of repairing splits in bentwood furniture. The
pieces marked (W) have to be hand fashioned to match
the curve you need for each job. These clamp heads
aren't coming out of nowhere, but are the heads of one
large "C" clamp, which is invisible because I am not the
world's most exciting drawer. But anyway, you get the
idea.*

DOWEL REPAIR OF SPLIT LONG BOWL

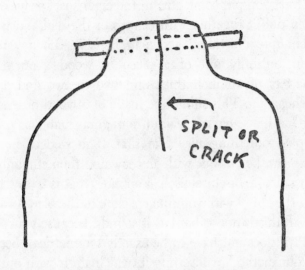

SPLIT OR CRACK

Of course, the split end must be clamped or wedged tight on a board while dowel hole is drilled and glue and dowel are inserted, but this is hard enough to do in real life without trying to draw both operations at once. So for the way to hold the split end together see the illustration and copy for Bellows just a page or two from here.

repair doesn't detract from the value of the bowl as an antique and in fact enhances its value a great deal. And even if you do a fairly sloppy job, that doesn't hurt either. Since it makes the patch look older and more "interesting."

First you put some glue in the crack just for luck, and then pull it together with clamps or the nail and wedge technique illustrated above in *Bellows*. Then you cut your butterfly out of a piece of wood about three-quarters of an inch thick and two to two and a half inches long. This should be made of a wood of reasonable hardness: cherry, walnut, Honduras mahogany, pear, apple—something nice like that. The wedges in your strip can be cut out with any saw and then straightened with a knife or chisel used as a knife (that is to say, holding the chisel with your fingers close to the blade).

All this is not as hard as it sounds, because your "butterfly" does not have to be exactly symmetrical, because of our method of inserting it, which starts with our cutting its outline onto the outside surface of the bowl. (Which incidentally remains clamped throughout this whole operation.)

Now, hollow out one side of the butterfly so that it fits snugly against the bowl, and glue it onto the outside of the bowl where the patch will be. This gluing is, of course, only temporary to keep the butterfly in place while you cut around its edges to start the hole that will receive it. Therefore for this temporary gluing you are

HOW TO
MAKE A
BUTTERFLY PATCH
IN A WOODEN BOWL.

PATCH IS TEMPORARILY
GLUED ON BOWL TO HELP
CUT MATCHING HOLE.
WITH EYACTO
KNIFE

ONCE PATCH FITS TIGHTLY
IT IS GLUED IN AND EXCESS
WOOD IS
SAND ED
OFF

The secret of figuring out what is going on here is more
or less explained in the text. If you are still puzzled,
write me a letter, and I'll come to your house and show
you what I mean.

best off with one of the rubber-base contact cements. These will hold firmly immediately, but you will still be able to pry the piece loose easily enough an hour or so later before it has completely cured.

The incision you make in the bowl around your butterfly should be made with a thin blade such as an Exacto knife, a single-edged razor blade or a very sharp penknife blade, and need only go about an eighth inch deep—but not less.

Now carefully pry loose your butterfly, and continue carving out the hole in your bowl that is going to receive it. This is obviously a slow and painstaking process because you have to be constantly careful to keep the fit snug as you go deeper into the bowl. Frankly, it is a good evening's work—about three hours—and if you aren't doing it because you enjoy this sort of thing you and I should never have gotten together in these pages in the first place.

The time to stop digging your excavation into the bowl is when the center of the outside surface of your butterfly is almost flush with the surface of the bowl at the crack. Then you glue it in—with Weldwood, of course—and the next day carve and sand it flush with the surface of the bowl.

Incidentally, partial or complete penetration of the butterfly patch through to the inside of the bowl is perfectly acceptable. You just need a fat enough butterfly,

The almost universal problem with hinges attaching box tops or lids is the splitting of the wood under the screws. Or around them. The secret is to get the dirty old glue out first by soaking it with vinegar. Then re-glue using a "C" clamp as shown about ten illustrations before this one. Finally, before screwing in new screw (of the exact right size, please) you pre-drill holes for them with a drill that is about half as wide as the screw. Try it out on a piece of scrap wood. Take your time. If you're in a hurry, I shouldn't even be talking to you.

and by the time you have cut all the way through the tightness of your fit is likely to be pretty questionable.

BOXES

Boxes? Well, it all depends on what kind of a box you're talking about, doesn't it? The only problem that I can think of that a box has that is inherent in its being a box is that the hinges have pulled out. And don't they always? So why don't you just check back to the entry on *Blanket Chests* for the principles involved? That leaves you only with the problem of finding small hinges, for which see the Appendix in the back of the book.

BRASSES

See accompanying illustration.

BREAD BOARDS (and Breadboard Table Tops)

Splitting is the problem here, because the main board shrinks laterally, and the end pieces don't shrink longitudinally. Happily, by the time your bread board is old enough to be of interest to us antique lovers such shrinking is completed. So all you have to do is pry the ends off, pull out the old nails, clamp the split center board tight and nail your end-pieces back.

If you are reproducing a bread board top and using

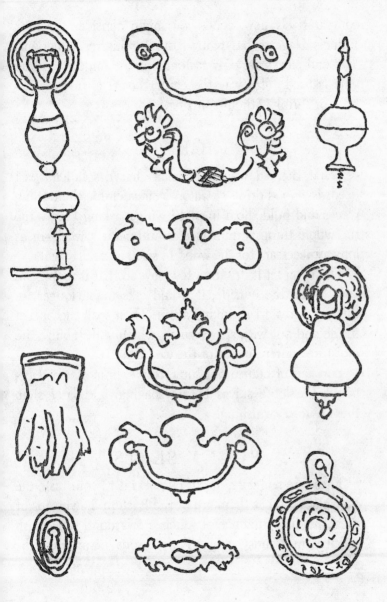

comparatively new wood, you might consider the trick
Francis Hagerty has figured out for his reproductions.
The end-pieces are only fastened in the middle, and no
glue is used. This way the center board is free to contract or shrink without splitting.

BUCKETS

What the old wooden bucket that has fallen apart
needs is a good drink of water. You assemble the rattling
pieces and hold them in place with masking tape while
the whole thing is immersed in water for a week—or as
long as necessary for the wood to swell up really tight.

Then you let it dry for a few days so that it feels good
and dry on the outside; it would take much longer for
the wood to start shrinking again. Then soak the bucket
inside and out with spar varnish, which will stabilize the
moisture content inside of the wood.

You can of course put some thin splints of wood between the loose staves before soaking, and later stain
these before varnishing.

BUGGY SEATS

These are real cute, and if cuteness is to your taste the
best places to get them are in the Eastern Townships of
the Canadian Province of Quebec or around the Amish
country in Pennsylvania. The reasons being that the

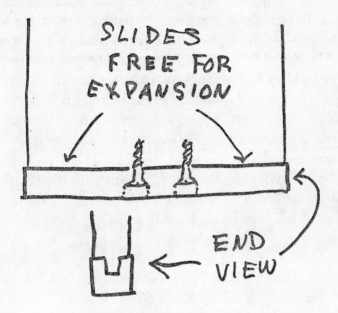

SLIDES
FREE FOR
EXPANSION

END
VIEW

The way to prevent wooden panels from cracking is to let them float free to expand or contract. Mostly contract—from drying out, of course. The simplest example is this breadboard table top, in which the end pieces are only fastened in the middle. You find panels that have to "float" free on all four edges in the sides of chests of drawers. They get glued into their slots by excess varnish or paint. Damned hard to fix without disassembling the whole side.

Eastern Townships are the places people have most recently stopped using buggies and that the Amish still do. In fact, there is a fellow in the business of buying buggies in Canada, trucking them to Pennsylvania on an old automobile carrier a dozen at a time, painting them a nice black and selling them to the Amish.

Consisting of iron frames with wooden seats and backs, these seats, after being detached from their buggies, are too low to sit on comfortably, and the most attractive and steadiest way to raise them is to mount them on a box built to size. This gives you a sort of magazine shelf under the seat. Or you can put a removable lid on your box for a nice shallow storage space to hide your good bottles of whiskey.

Carriage striping will doll these things up a bit, as will a red velvet cushion. Then your house will look just like a sham English pub on Route 66.

CANE

As any fool can plainly tell you, once caning has been damaged in any way the only solution is to replace the whole panel or section of it. Well, I'll tell you right now that any fool is plainly wrong. And has been ever since the white glues (such as the widely distributed Elmer's) have been on the market.

Because when cane is soaked in and coated with this kind of glue, the cane can be restored to ninety-five and maybe a hundred percent of its original strength. Of course to make these repairs you need patience, two blocks of flat wood a little larger than the size of the damaged area and some sheets of waxed paper to face the blocks of wood to keep the glue from sticking to the blocks when they are pressing the cane flat from both sides. A great big C-clamp is also useful to press the blocks together while the glue is drying. But you can also use hand pressure, as the glue sets in about ten minutes and you can easily last ten minutes with your hands if you relax them for fifteen seconds every two or three minutes during that time.

That is the general principle involved, and there are so many possible variations in the size and shape of the damage, I don't think it appropriate to go into specific instructions for them all. But here are some more generalities that might help:

First of all, no matter how bad the damage looks at first glance, I assure you that if you take the time to look at it and think about it, you will see that it can be repaired by breaking it down into steps, that is into three or four gluing sessions. In the first session you may want to glue together just the ends of a few broken strands to establish your restored position.

This is done by gluing the ends together while holding them in place by pinning them both to a small block of wood (insulated from the glue by a small piece of wax paper, of course).

The next session you can glue together some strands running at right angles to the ones already glued. As you go along excess glue can be sliced off with a single-edged razor blade or even better a pointed Exacto knife. I'll admit that it's picky-picky-picky all the way, but if you don't like this sort of thing why don't you take up bridge or bowling?

I suppose the most common problem with caning is a sagging bottom that has begun to give along one edge. In this case what you do is establish the seat of the chair upside down on a waterproof table top (or one suitably covered with a plastic sheet or other waterproof covering). Then you soften the cane by soaking it with wet toweling placed on it. Depending on the cane you will have to keep this toweling wet for from twenty-four hours to four days. When the cane is as soft and pliable as it is going to get, you dry it and push it back into position and weight it down to dry flat. You achieve this by covering it with dry toweling and weighting that down with blocks of wood on which you stack books, gallon cans of paint or whatever. This can take an annoyingly long time, and you start out changing the toweling for fresh dry toweling every half hour, then every four hours, then over night. But you can speed up the process by heating your toweling first on a hot radiator. You can probably get your cane dry in four hours by applying fresh hot, dry toweling every ten minutes. Or you can try ironing it through a towel with a hand iron set for "cotton."

When the cane is dry, you soak the whole seat in your white glue for fifteen minutes so it will penetrate the cane. Then you wipe it off with a damp rag, and press it flat to dry over night between two sheets of waxed paper.

You did this just to firmly establish the position of the cane. After twenty-four hours you peel the wax paper off, and trim any excess glue off with your Exacto knife. Another picky-picky job on which you should be reconciled to spending an hour and a half. But then you are ready to brush on a final coating of glue, top, and bottom, which you cannot allow to air dry. No more waxed paper! Depending on how thick your first coat was, you may want to go for the insurance by applying a second coating of glue after another forty-eight hours of drying time. And I think you should. After all, what have you got to show for your time if you waste it playing bridge or going bowling?

Now having said all that about repairs I still realize that there will undoubtedly be times when you will want to replace old caning with new. In that event, there are two companies which will supply you not only with everything you need, but also very good booklets of instructions on how to do caning from scratch. And since you are going to have to buy your cane from them anyway, there is no point in my reproducing their directions which are better than I could write anyhow.

In each case you ought to send along about fifty cents for their catalogues of supplies and direction booklets. These companies are:

THE H. H. PERKINS COMPANY
10 South Bradley Road
Woodbridge, Connecticut 06525

and

SAVIN HANDCRAFTS
P. O. Box 4251
Hamden, Connecticut 55514

Both of these companies are wonderfully friendly and helpful, but they have terrible slogan writers. One of them (Savin) knocks me right off my chair with "Weaving kits for all ages!" And the other one (Perkins) is right in there counterpunching with "A chair is only as good as the seat that is in it!" But I shouldn't complain. It's nice to know that there are some real people left in this world.

CASTERS

Aside from oiling the main problem with these is that one is missing and what you need is a new matching set of four. Wise old antique dealers and junk shops save these sets from junked pieces just for this purpose and will sell them to you cheaply. For reproductions of brass

ones see the catalogue section in the back of the book.
Porcelain ones are also available out of stocks left over
from Victorian furniture factories, and you will find
these advertised from time to time in the pages of THE
ANTIQUE TRADER.

CHAIRS

Chairs with curved pieces in them present the worst
problems, and the only way to repair them is with
dowels, for which see illustration herewith and refer
back to *Woodworking* in the introduction to this chapter.

For all old chairs the problem is that they start falling
apart because until a few decades ago nobody had invented a decent glue. The so-called hide, fish and hoof
glues—all the ones that look like a thick maple syrup—
and the ones you have to melt, just have no resistance at
all to moisture in the air on damp days. So the only right
way to re-glue a chair is to take it apart as much as possible by knocking it with a leather mallet or padded hammer. Then the old glue can be softened rapidly by soaking it with vinegar for about fifteen minutes. And you
just scrape it off with a chisel and a penknife to get into
any dowel holes.

When re-gluing (with Weldwood, of course) be sure
to make all the joints fit tightly by driving little wedges
of wood into any space they will fit into, then cut the

protruding ends off with a razor blade for a neat job. All glue works best if it gets to dry under pressure, and this is especially true of the end of rungs fitting into chair legs. For this purpose someone has invented a strap clamp—like a big cinch-buckle belt. Or you can use rope and twist it tight with a stick. A sort of chair tourniquet.

There is a device around like a sort of glue hypodermic needle that you use to squirt glue into joints that you have drilled small holes in from the side of the leg. But these are a delusion because you haven't removed the old glue, which will crumble again in a few more years, and the new glue can't get at the bare wood to do its work.

Often you will want to re-glue a chair with an upholstered seat without going to all the work of removing all the upholstery so you can knock the frame apart. And, strangely enough, this can be done quite well. You just pry off the edging strip and pull up the corners of the seat cover. You scrape as much old glue out of the now exposed joints as you can. Push in what new glue you can, tie or clamp and let the glue dry. This is, of course, a lousy job, but it is enough to hold your pieces of chair together rigidly while you do the real trick. And this is to drill holes across the joints and fasten them with fresh dowels—the ends of which wherever possible will be covered when you tack your seat covering and edging back in place again. Exposed dowel ends are cut off and sanded flush. Then you stain them and conceal them with touch-up powders and spray lacquer.

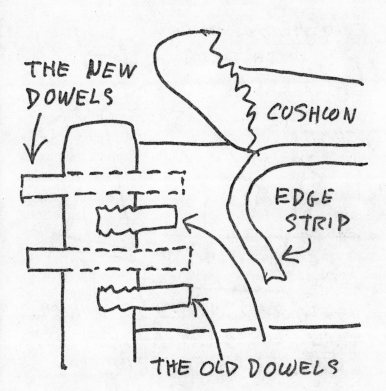

THE NEW
DOWELS

CUSHION

EDGE
STRIP

THE OLD DOWELS

Of course, you clean and re-glue the old dowels first, and
let the glue set overnight. But then to get a really
guaranteed job, you drill two new holes right through
the front face of the chair leg, and insert two new
dowels. Naturally, the protruding ends have to be cut
off, and the front face of the leg has to be restored with
some filler and touch-up powders. Well, I never
promised you a rose garden.

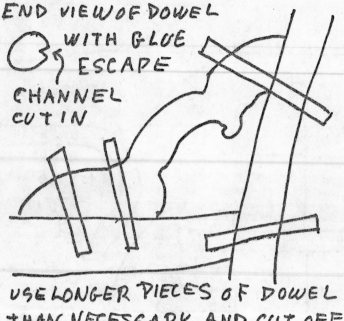

END VIEW OF DOWEL
WITH GLUE
ESCAPE
CHANNEL
CUT IN

USE LONGER PIECES OF DOWEL
THAN NECESSARY AND CUT OFF
ENDS AFTER HAMMERING IN.

You can do wonders with dowel repairing on even the most complicated angles and curves. Of course you have to figure out where to put your dowels on each different piece, and the hard part is figuring ways to clamp the irregular pieces together tightly while you are drilling the dowel holes. It's the sort of thing you have to enjoy doing, or you'd go mad.

CHERRY TABLES (etc.)

The repair of tables in general is taken up later in this chapter, but the Early American drop-leaf table is such a popular piece that it is somehow in a class by itself, and there are also some things to be said about cherry wood.

The reason there were so many cherry tables made from colonial days almost up to the Civil War is that cherry was the middle class man's substitute for the Honduras mahogany used in the furniture of the rich people in Philadelphia, New York and Boston. Some of it made in those cities, some imported from England.

So all these early cherry tables were originally stained a dark red, as opposed to the lighter browns or natural that everyone seems to prefer today. And, so stained, you have to cross the room and look at the figure in the wood closely to tell the difference.

About every house in the country must have had one of these tables until the coming of the Victorian era. And then these gems were considered to be out of style. So they were replaced by golden oak monstrosities and demoted to the kitchen or cooking shed or even the cellar workshop.

That is why they are often found covered with black water marks, dirty oil soaked into them, and marked with circular indentations on the edges of their top from meat grinders and other contraptions having been screwed onto them. And with tops and leaves warped.

Happily cherry is the most reclaimable or restorable of all woods. WITHOUT sanding and thus losing the character of the worn and used surface unless absolutely necessary! Sanding any antique wood unless totally necessary is the mark of the Visigoth and other direct descendants from cretin man.

Some of the cures for these special ills of cherry tables are as follows:

The warps come out beautifully with cherry by putting the concave side down on a flat grassy lawn on a sunny summer day for an hour, more or less. (I speak as a New Englander. In autumn or spring it just takes longer, and in Southern California or Florida winter is just as good.) But this will take a few trys on a few days due to a slight tendency for a flattened leaf to regress to its warp over night in your house. Or you often over-correct a warp and have to briefly reverse the process a little. That's not as hard as it sounds, because it is great fun, and everybody in your neighborhood will be fascinated and come over to ask you what the hell you're doing.

The black marks from water—a blemish to which cherry is outstandingly susceptible—come out like magic when you soak them (after scrubbing off any surface grease with soap and water or finish remnants with paint remover) with a saturate solution of oxalic acid crystals in water or denatured alcohol. The basic proce-

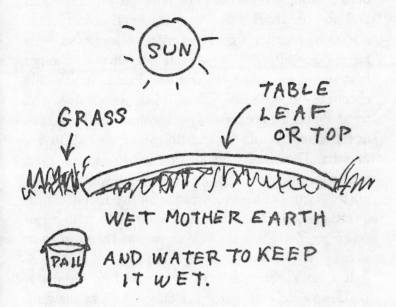

You really should put off taking warps out of table tops and leaves until a good hot sunny August day because the trick works so much faster with a really broiling sun. With pine in an hour or two, with the dense wood in maybe only one full day. But I have seen wood that took three days to straighten out even in a good hot sun. In any event, you will want to keep good old wet mother earth good and wet by lifting up your table leaf, etc., every hour or so and pouring a pail of water on it. Also you can put rocks on top, or on the high corners in case of a twisted warp.

dure is to fill a milk bottle or equivalent with hot water and pour in about a quarter of a pound box of oxalic acid crystals or until no more crystals dissolve on shaking. (This stuff will sting in scratches but otherwise not hurt your bare fingers. In this case "acid" means only chemically opposite of "alkali," like vinegar is.) The wood should be good and dry, of course, so it will suck in the liquid. Works fast. In thirty-nine seconds to five minutes. Then flush off with clear water, wipe dry, and neutralize any traces of oxalic in the wood with a bath of pure vinegar. Let the vinegar soak for five minutes, then give the wood a final rinse with water—like from a garden hose. You get oxalic acid crystals at any *good* paint store.

If some Victorian ancestor has cleaned his carburator on the top of your particular table, you can draw up some of the oil with a hot iron and blotting paper—after a good soap and water scrubbing, of course. This will leave you still fairly unhappy, but it is a necessary first step. The next step, which should be obvious to the meanest intelligence, is to soak the whole top of the table and both leaves with dirty oil from your crankcase or the drum down at your gas station. In other words, you don't remove the stain—because you can't—you match it. It's a matter of when you can't beat 'em, join 'em.

Now to further equalize appearances, remove the oil with a bath of weak lye water. That's about a half can of lye crystals to two quarts of water. Scrub this in a lot with an old fashioned bristle scrubbing brush. In addition to removing the oil, this will also turn the cherry wood a delightful brown, making it quite unnecessary to stain the wood before finishing.

Now flush and wipe your lye-water solution off the wood, neutralize any lye in the surface with a bath of vinegar, flush with water and let dry. If there is a fuzz on the surface of the wood after all this, rub it off with "oo" grade steel wool, and you can now proceed with staining the wood even darker if you wish and then finishing.

For those who like their cherry wood lighter than it looks after a lye bath, this lye-given brownness can easily be removed by using a liquid laundry bleach as a neutralizing bath instead of the vinegar. It only takes a few minutes for the bleach to work. Then flush it off with clear water.

There are reasons for all this neutralizing and flushing with clear water. Any traces of lye left in the wood's surface will cause gummy spots in any finish you apply over them. Traces of oxalic acid will turn pink under the finish as it dries. Traces of the laundry bleach will affect any stain you might apply.

There are two schools of thought about the signs of wear and marks of abuse. Some people try to conceal them as much as possible by scratching them out, staining them, filling them with patching sticks and concealing them with touch-up powders. Other people like to let their cherry tables wear their marks like badges of honor. The second group is right, because telling stories of what has happened in the past is what antiques are all about. It is beyond being a matter of what is ugly and what is beautiful. Marks left by meat-grinders on cherry tables in 1880 are history. And when you try to change history, you're crazy.

CHESTS OF DRAWERS

Sometimes when I think of the sorrows and ailments that can beset a poor chest of drawers I could almost cry. Especially an Empire chest drawers, because they were designed and made so terribly. But we take those special problems up in the *Empire* listing under *Furniture Styles*. Here we are concerned only with common ills such as sticking drawers, loose or missing knobs and pulls, rattling drawers, musty smells and ordinary falling apart.

Starting with the worst first, the only right way to re-glue a chest of drawers is to knock it all apart so it lies around the floor like a kit. The reason for spreading it out is to be able to remember which piece came from where as you will find out that in anything antique, left side pieces are rarely interchangeable with right side pieces. Nor are the different drawers ever the same size or even shape.

Which brings me to an important tip that I learned

the hard way. When you re-glue any "box" that contains drawers you are in danger of finding, after everything is dry, that all your drawers are a quarter of an inch bigger than the spaces they are supposed to fit in. This is due to shrinkage of the wood and that you have taken up all the slack with your re-gluing. Also you can find that your drawers tilt imperceptibly one way and your chest imperceptibly the other. Imperceptible, that is, until you try to get the drawers back in.

The answer is to be sure you have the drawers back in their proper spaces while the glue in your box joints is drying. And then make sure your drawers fit into their spaces before their glue dries. Or at least almost fit, because you usually have to trim them down a little. The big thing is for your box to dry straight.

Sticking drawers is caused by warping of the drawer sides or some other uneven ratio of drying in all the little pieces of wood involved, and if rubbing paraffin on likely spots doesn't solve the problem some trimming with a plane will have to be done.

When drawers are loose, first check and if necessary refasten the guides inside the chest. More frequently, especially if the wood is pine, the bottoms of the drawer sides will have chaffed away and/or worn grooves in the pieces of wood that support them. There is nothing easy to be done about this. It is a lot of fussy work, but you are just going to have to glue thin strips of new wood to the bottom edges of the drawers and replace the supporting pieces inside the box.

But the most common complaint of all is a chest of drawers with a musty (or worse) smell. Washing it out with soap and water may get them clean, but it doesn't help the smell. What you have to do is seal the smell in, and there are two approaches to this. The first is to soak every square inch of surface of both the box and the drawers with "boiled" linseed oil. This isn't really boiled, but just has a japan drier added to it. (If you try boiling your own linseed oil you are going to end up burning down your house.) The result is a chest of drawers that smells of linseed oil. But some people think that is great. Since I don't, I apply a good thick coat of shellac (two parts shellac to one part denatured alcohol thinner) to all inside surfaces.

If you are troubled with worms, ticks or dry rot, you soak all surfaces—outside as well as inside—with a product called Cuprinol. This is a base of petroleum distillate (like mineral spirits or turpentine) and won't hurt any exterior finishes. After a good soaking, wipe off, let dry and then seal it in with shellac inside. If you can't get Cuprinol in your local paint and hardware store, they always carry it in boatyards, for dry rot in wooden hulls.

For missing brass pulls and knobs, see the catalogue section in the back of the book. Wooden knobs are usually impossible to match or even find. Ideally these can be turned on a lathe, but who has a lathe? The alternative is to rough out a knob on a power saw and with a disc sander, then hold it in a vice while you finish it off with hand tools: knife, chisel, wood rasp, file, penknife. The best way to do this is to shape your knob on the end of a piece of wood about eight inches long so you have something to hold onto while you work on your knob, leaving the cutting of the knob off the end of the stick for your last step.

CLOCKS

If you think a foolish consistency is going to stop me from telling you the right way to clean a clock, you don't know me very well, because inconsistencies are just about my favorite thing in the world. The main "secret" is that you use benzine, which just happens to be lighter fluid. And if you are suspicious of that, you can also get benzine at a drug store for twice the price. Obviously you soak the works if possible, but you can also flush and brush.

The second "secret" is that once clean you oil it with *nothing but* clock oil, which you have to get from your local watchmaker or Mason & Sullivan (see below).

And the really good secret is that you don't oil the cogs of the gears—just the bearings. And you do that with a needle stuck into the eraser on the end of a pencil

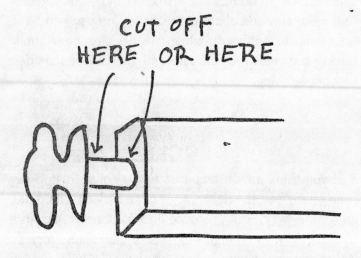

The way you whittle a new knob—whether you speed
up the job with a power sander or not—is work on one
end of a stick so you have something to hold onto. You
do the knob first, its dowel section second. Or if you
want a dowelless knob, just cut it off the end of your
stick with a saw.

so that you can get the tiniest amount of oil possible into the bearing—the more oil the more dust to be caught in it.

Now about Mason & Sullivan. This is the mail-order branch of a great clock company, so besides selling you oil, they also carry things like brass finials, hands, all kinds of faces, foot levelers, weights and replacement movements that are spring, weight, electric and battery operated. Even a reproduction of an old moving moon face for a grandfather clock (around $60).

COBBLER'S BENCH

Whether a detailed one used by a professional cobbler or one of the simple rough ones that every farmhouse had and used up to about 1900, these benches all have one problem in common. And that is that the legs get loose where they were inserted in a hole in the seat plank and then the top of the leg was split and expanded with a wooden wedge. And since the wood has usually gotten punky just squirting some glue in the cracks won't work very well.

For a good job knock the leg out of its hole with a hammer. Working from the bottom, chisel away the soft wood. Scrape the dirt and old glue off the top of the leg, and put it back in with a couple of wedges to hold it at the right angle. Soak the open surfaces around the top of the leg with Weldwood glue. And finally stuff the spaces with a putty made by mixing sawdust into about a half a cup of Weldwood glue. When this putty has dried it hardens to the strength of hard oak, and can be sanded or ground or filed smooth.

DECORATIONS

By "decorations" I mean the flat-backed carvings or mouldings that are glued and nailed with small brads to the surfaces of furniture. The French went big for this in their Louis and Regency styles. The Adams brothers picked it up in England; then you find it a lot in our own Renaissance Victorian.

Naturally, you aren't going to be able to find stuff like this in your run of the mill hardware store in East Punkin, Vermont, or probably even in Rutland. You have to get to a city big enough to have some interior decorators in it, because they are the ones that use a lot of this stuff. Then if you are a friendly person, you can ask a decorator where he goes. If not, look in the "yellow pages" under *Wood Products* and *Woodworkers*.

There is one mail-order house that I know of that has a limited line of these things, and that is Constantine. See Appendix for a description of their catalogue and address.

A lot of the classic styles of furniture (and their good
Grand Rapids reproductions) have glued on decorations
that look like carved wood, but are actually cast out of
fine sawdust and some kind of glue. At any rate, if you
are missing one of these you can get them from the
Constantine mail-order catalogue. (See Appendix.) The
above are just a small sampling. If you can't find an
exact match, knock the other one off and get two.

DESKS

All the constructional problems you run across in desks are the same as those found in *Chests of Drawers* and *Blanket Chests* for which see listings above. For the special hardware used to lower some of the slant fronts, see the catalogue section in the back of the book.

DRY SINKS

For general construction problems see *Blanket Chests* and *Chests of Drawers*. The old ones are pretty scarce, but you can still find a few in the Back Kingdom of Maine, and in the spring they still come into Defoy in the Province of Quebec.

FLOORS

I don't think the inclusion of floors in a book on restoring antiques is too far-fetched. After all, houses get to be antiques and people who care about antiques usually commit the ultimate folly of buying an antique house sooner or later. Besides, I know something interesting about old floors. Straight ammonia will dissolve the original bloodmilk paint on the old pine floors of Early American farm houses. Of course you have to use it in the summer with the windows open and preferably wearing a gas mask. But you don't have to mop up the gunk afterward. You just lean in the window with a garden hose and flush it down the cracks. That's good for the foundation. Tightens it up. Annoys the hell out of termites, too. And you can do the same thing with water-solvent paint removers for more recent layers of paint. This will give you floors that are a lot more authentic than if you sand them down, which is an atrocious thing to do to a really historic house.

The most frustrating problem with old pine floors is the way the cracks between the old wide boards keep opening and closing. The expansion of the boards in summer and contraction of them in winter works loose any filler put into the cracks—that is if you are a compulsive type that wants a floor sanded perfectly smooth. The trouble is that you are asking wide pine boards to be something that they aren't. And what is so terrible about having open spaces between old wide pine boards, for heavens sake?

What we used to do—and you still could—was to fill them with a putty made by mixing sawdust with a mixture of half black paint and half spar varnish. You don't try to bring this up to level, but push it in until you have shallow culverts running between the boards. This mixture is elastic enough so that the opening of any new cracks will be rare.

But if you can stand the incredible cost of it, there is now on the market a modern caulking compound under a variety of trade names that is the perfect material for this job. Their generic name is "phenolic caulking compounds," and the one we get in New England is typically called Phenoseal, which you get through paint and hardware stores or at boatyards. This lovely stuff comes in regular caulking-gun cartridges in white, gray and black, black being the one for floor cracks. It squirts in easily, sticks completely, and remains permanently flexible when dry—in twenty-four hours. The only trouble is that it costs (at this writing, and I'm sure things will get worse) two dollars a cartridge, and I used up ten on the last old wideboard kitchen floor I fixed up!

Assuming you have a sanded floor—and I suppose I have to accept the fact that this is what most people prefer—you are naturally going to want to varnish it. Well, don't. Modern varnishes are a great tough film, but they don't work on soft old pine. They work on oak and maple fine, but on soft pine they indent and crack every time you lean back in a chair. For soft old pine you need the kind of wood sealers that are sold for use on basketball courts, usually indicated by incorporating the word "gym" in their names. This stuff sinks deep into the surface of old pine. In fact the pine sucks it in like a sponge. So two or three coats are necessary. But the result is a floor that looks like pine, but wears like iron. Well anyway, oak. On top of this you should naturally use Old English floor wax.

FRAMES, GILDED

It comes as a shock to some people to find out that their ornate gilded frames are really made out of plaster of paris and aren't carved out of wood. Well that's the way it goes. If you go back to the fifteenth century in Italy, they were carved out of wood alright, but even those had to be faced with plaster of paris (or the local fine clay equivalent) to give them a smooth enough surface to take gold leaf—which needs a *very* smooth surface so that it can be burnished without rubbing off.

And then by Victorian times in the United States (and anywhere else I guess) the mass production boys just made solid plaster castings of the most ornate shapes and glued them onto plain frames. Or the whole face may be plaster, in which case the plain wooden frame was pressed into the plaster while it was still wet in the mould.

As to repairing these, broken-off pieces glue back easily enough with ordinary white glue. It is replacing missing parts that is the tricky business. If it is a small piece you can sculpt it out of artist's modeling clay of the kind that air dries. And if this falls off when it has dried, you just glue it back on with white glue. Of course, that clay takes several days to dry, so if you are in a hurry, you can make a plaster of paris paste that takes about fifteen minutes to set by mixing it up with a solution of one-third vinegar and two-thirds water. Both can be made smooth enough with very fine sandpaper and the "ooo" grade steel wool to take gold leaf.

Larger sections are replaced by making moulds of the matching area on the other side of the frame, using an impression taken with the waxy kind of modeling clay and pouring plaster of paris into it.

Before applying gold leaf, the smoothed surface must be sized with two coats of shellac or clear spray lacquer. The first will sink in, and needs to dry for two hours. The second or third—will stay on the surface, and you polish this again with "ooo" steel wool.

Applying the gold leaf turns out to be amazingly easy. You get your gold leaf (or the cheaper imitation) and "gold size" (a varnishy "glue") at your art supply store. Now you brush the thinnest possible coat of size on the plaster with a camel's hair brush, and let it dry for forty-five minutes. Then you lay the gold leaf on as illustrated, tamp it down with cotton balls and burnish it with them too. You can then spray on a protective coating of lacquer if you want to, but it will take away from the quality of the reflection of the uncoated stuff.

And I want to repeat that regardless of how it sounds, this is not hard. I think anyone can do it the first time on a "carved" frame. However, you do have to practice to develop a skill at it if you want to do large flat surfaces that don't show any imperfections.

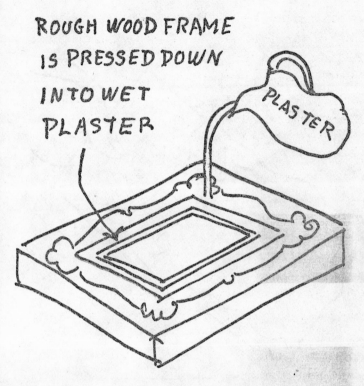

ROUGH WOOD FRAME
IS PRESSED DOWN
INTO WET
PLASTER

PLASTER

They started out with rubbing clay or plaster on the face
of carved wooden frames so they would be smooth
enough to take gold-leafing. And they ended up in
Victorian times by casting the whole thing out of plaster
of paris with pieces of wood pushed down into the
plaster while it was still wet to reinforce the plaster. And
there are all kinds of variations between these two
extremes.

This isn't really a piece of gold leaf—as deceptive as my drawing may be—but a piece of imitation gold leaf, sometimes called Dutch metal. It's a lot cheaper and easier to handle because it comes in a pack with tissue sheets in between. This drawing shows how you lay it down on your sized surface with a piece of cardboard that you pull out from under it. It's very fragile.

FURNITURE STYLES

Many problems a restorer faces with wooden furniture are not derived from the use to which a piece was put, but from the way things were made and decorated in the period of its origin. Some of those problems that easily derive from style or period are as follows:

Chinese. For the typical highly polished lacquer finish see listing for *Chinese Lacquer* under *Finishes* in Part I of this book. Another area of difficulty lies in the construction of chairs, tables and small folding tables that have been a standard item of export from China—and lately Hong Kong—for the last three centuries.

The outstanding problem about these pieces is that they are fitted together out of pieces of wood that have been impregnated with oil to such a degree that when anything breaks you can't repair it with glue. Not even Weldwood is going to stick to oil, so don't bother trying. You have to think of these things as metal and repair them the way a garage mechanic would: with nuts and bolts and strap metal screwed tight with steel screws into carefully drilled holes. This is the one situation in which you can repair wooden things with metal, because this oil impregnated wood seems to be so stable that it has about the same coefficient of expansion as steel. Or brass, which is more attractive if your repair has to show.

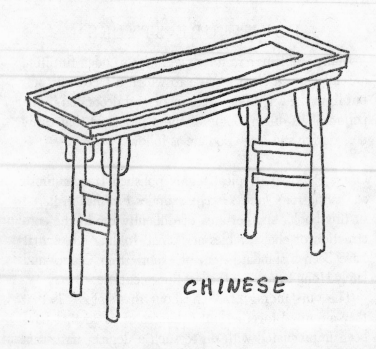

CHINESE

People who have worked in the Orient tend to bring these home. And the reason there are so many of them around is that a lot more people work in the Orient than you realize until you stop to think about it. For instance: State Department people, CIA assassins, Flying Tiger pilots, heroin importers, oh, sure! And the English brought them home by the boatload, and are now sending them over here in their $7,000 "containers" of antiques.

Looks a lot more Chinese than steel, and if you grind the corners round, brass strap repairs look as if they might have been done in China a hundred years ago. Gives your piece a special *cachet*.

The most common of these pieces are the small folding tables with round tops. Almost all of these have black lacquered tops with Chinese style pictures made of metal pieces fitted into the surface with great precision. Once this black lacquer has become cloudy and spotted by too many spilt martinis it can be restored by padding it with lacquer amalgamator or sometimes ordinary lacquer thinner.

But if you go all the way and remove all the black lacquer, you will find that under it is a beautiful teak-like wood. It has the same striped figure only curvier—and that anyone would prefer this to be covered by black lacquer is one of the great mysteries of the Orient. Of course, if such a table is an important, really antique one of museum quality you would have to put back the black lacquer. But at the rate these things have been produced and sold to tourists this would be a one in a million possibility. And if you have any cause to suspect that you have such a treasure in hand any museum curator will be glad to advise you.

This wood is so hard and dense that only one coat of varnish or wood sealer is needed to give it a very strong alcohol-proof finish, but I suppose two coats aren't going to hurt.

COTTAGE PINE

Real Early American furniture ran out years ago. There just wasn't enough of it, so by now it is all in museums or owned by very rich people. But fortunately a lot of pine was used in the early mass-produced furniture of the post-Civil War period—and up until as late as the early 1900's. Much of it being sold through Sears & Roebuck catalogue. And since it was pine, all you have to do is scrape it down, stain it, and add some scroll work to have a pretty good imitation.

Cottage Pine. This is the name given to the first mass-produced furniture that was the furniture of the common man from around 1850 until our factories started turning out oak in the early 1900's. It was always painted, false-grained and decorated with neat little paintings of flowers or sheaves of wheat or other nature motifs. You can still easily find complete bedroom sets of this sort of thing with the original decoration, which at this point in history is more worth preserving than scraping off to reveal the aged pine underneath. But such scraping has been going on for decades, and accounts for ninety-eight percent of the so-called Early American Pine found in antique shops. The most obvious way to distinguish this scraped stuff is that the chest pieces and commodes have paneled sides, whereas the really early stuff has plank sides of one wide board. The second most obvious distinction is that the drawers of the mass-produced stuff have obviously machine-cut dovetails whereas the old stuff has hand-cut dovetails and only three or four to a side at that.

When you find such a piece that hasn't been scraped down and converted to "Early American," you can usually restore the original decoration to its original pristine condition with startling success. This is because the original ground painting and false graining were done with water-base paints and then covered with a protective coating of shellac. All the dirt and grime on the piece are naturally on the shellac, and this can be carefully wiped off with denatured alcohol without disturbing the paint underneath it. The only place you have to watch your step is with the little painted bunches of flowers. These were done in oil paints, and the shellac must be removed from them by gently brushing the denatured alcohol on them with a camel's hair brush and blotting up the dissolved shellac with little pads of cotton.

As the manufacture of such pieces continued into the Victorian era they were made more and more in the Victorian style with walnut mouldings tacked on to imitate or at least suggest Victorian Renaissance (Civil War era) walnut. These pieces restore just as easily as the earlier ones and unquestionably should be restored whenever possible rather than scraped down to the pine.

In the case that such a piece has been painted over, it is impossible to remove the paint without destroying the original decoration. Unless you go about it a quarter of a square inch at a time the way valuable paintings are restored, and this is impracticable.

The most interesting of these pieces is the lift-top commode because such pieces make nice little bars and cabinets for Early American record players. In fact there is such a demand for them that these are being widely reproduced in many a little woodworking mill in New England—in pine, and sold unfinished. There are also curvey reproductions being made by the big furniture companies in maple which is patently ridiculous. As are

all maple reproductions of Early American things that
were originally only made in pine.

Early American. The term "early" is obviously relative.
But for purposes of communication we mean by this furniture and other wooden things made in this country before the advent of factory production. But since early is
relative we already have a few exceptions. The first is
the early spool beds that were turned on a lathe (driven
by foot-power or a water wheel) but otherwise cut out
and assembled by hand. The other is the Hitchcock and
other fancy chairs made in the earliest American factories in reflection of the Sheraton style of our Revolu-
tionary period.

Which brings up the point that any furniture made in
the United States in imitation of established English
styles may be Early American, but is called by its style
prefixed with "American." And as these were all made
by the big city cabinetmakers for the rich, what we have
left to be called simply Early American is the country-
made furniture made by small-town cabinetmakers and
farmers for their own families during the winter months
to take advantage of that time in which there was nothing else left to do in the barn.

That this stuff made by so many unrelated people has
a certain over-all style is based on two factors. First was
the limited number of things you could do to pine

boards with the primitive tools they had to use. The second is that they often made some effort to make their pieces look at least something like the furniture they saw either on their trips to the cities or in engravings. A perfect example of this is the country-made Windsor chairs, of which there are seemingly no two alike, but all look something like the original English model. (Undoubtedly sets were made, but it is rare to find them intact.)

The main point from a restorer's point of view (after repairing broken pieces which is discussed elsewhere) is that since these pieces were always made with some idea of more refined style in mind, they were always painted to conceal the "common" pine of which they were basically made.

I have already said the basic technical thing about this in a previous entry in this chapter, *Milk Paint* under *Finishes*. So go look that over and come back.

The point I want to make here is that such original paint—plain or false grained—has been stripped off for so many years that any of it you can find now is worth more than its weight in gold. In fact, all such pieces that are newly discovered really belong in museums. And so the restoration of such a piece is worth a lot of time and care. What I am especially referring to is when such a piece has been covered with one or more additional coats of paint over the years.

As the more recent coats will most likely be of an oil-base paint and the original coat of a milk paint, the oil-

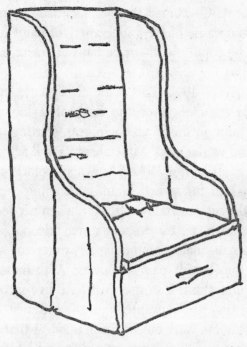

EARLY AMERICAN

Of course, the rich people of the Colonial period
imported their furniture from England—or had it made
by English cabinetmakers who had come over to
Philadelphia and New York. But out in the country
carpenters were using their winter months to make
simple "primitive" things such as this combination
chair and chest.

base paints can be removed with little damage to the original coat. Of course there is no exact formula for doing this because of the wide variety of paint formulas you may be coping with—or perhaps attacking is a better word.

All you can do is start with an obscure area—the lower side of a chest or the back of a leg—and try different solutions in square-inch areas, starting with the mildest and working up. Mineral spirits will actually dissolve some asphaltum (black-brown in color) paints if left to soak in for several hours by keeping a piece of cloth on the surface and re-wetting it when needed.

Other things to try are denatured alcohol, lacquer thinner, amalgamator, ammonia, lye, waterbase and volatile (acetone-based) paint removers. With these timing becomes important. You may just have five seconds between the time the unwanted paint is softened and the solution starts to work on the finish under it that you are trying to preserve. So you must be prepared to blot up, flush off or neutralize your active agent in that time.

Paper towels are fine for blotting up which is all that you do with: mineral spirits, alcohol, lacquer thinner and amalgamator.

Ammonia must first be flushed off with a solution of half water and half vinegar. This can easily be applied from a pre-mixed jar of the solution with a soft two-inch paint brush. Then you blot.

Lye solution is first flushed with straight vinegar and then blotted up.

The water-base paint removers that the label instructs you to remove with water or just wipe off are either lye suspended in an emulsion or first cousins of lye. So here again you first flush with a half vinegar, half water solution before blotting up.

The volatile-base paint removers (strong fumes similar to lacquer thinner) are acetone combined with wax to prevent its immediate evaporation. So you will want to brush-flush these off with mineral spirits and then blot.

Don't be discouraged if what you uncover so painstakingly looks pretty ratty from the kicking around the piece got before it was painted. Amazing touch-up jobs can be done with such pieces if you first take the time to establish exact color matches. Artists' oil paints are the best for several reasons. They don't change color as they dry. You can wipe your mistakes off easily and they smudge well. And it is this smudging that is the key to all successful deception in touch-up work.

The point is to have no hard edges to arrest the eye of the observer. The basic technique is to apply a tiny amount of your paint with a camel's hair brush and then smudge in the proper direction with your finger tip. An alternative is to use artists' oil-painting brushes with what is called dry-brush technique, which in this case means having so little paint on your brushes that you have to press hard and "smudge" the paint on.

In working this way the oil paints are mixed as they come from the tube, and only thinned if needed with a drop of mineral spirits. After your work has dried—in twenty-four hours—the new paint will have a matte finish which will probably be different from the rest of the surface. This can be equalized and the whole surface protected by one or two thin coats of satin finish lacquer applied from a spray can. To change the subject, I am quite aware that in spite of all I keep saying about the value of original painted finishes on Early American pine, ninety-eight percent of everybody still prefers it stained an "antique brown" with a clear finish.

This antique brown color is actually about half way between brown mahogany and walnut, and an excellent combination stain and sealer in this color can be obtained by the gallon from Cohasset Colonials in Cohasset, Massachusetts. But if you are one of the two percent, you can get antique colors of paint for this purpose from Sturbridge Workshop, Sturbridge, Connecticut. Both places have catalogues.

Finally, some of this country-made furniture that best deserves the name Early American was also made in cherry and especially maple. Both are, of course, much more valuable than the pine because of their comparative rarity usually interesting figures in the wood. Even so they were mostly originally painted, though I have yet to see one in such original condition.

Empire. Originally designed and made in France in response to Napoleon's conquests, this furniture manages to express the nature of his "empire" very well. It looks massive, strong and dignified on the outside, and is punky and usually falling apart on the inside.

But as you will remember during the Revolution the French sided with us against the English. So after the war a craze for everything French swept our growing country, and so it came to pass that far more Empire was made in the United States than was made in France, which at the time was already full of furniture. Except for the famous poor people of Paris, of course, but they couldn't afford any. All they could even afford to eat was *cake*, a French word which best translates to our "hardtack," which has given us history's most famous misquotation. What Marie Antoinette really said wasn't, "let them eat cake." What she actually said was, "If they have no bread, let them eat hardtack." Which is still kind of heartless, but not crazy.

To get back to the point, the trouble with this stuff is that it consists of blocky pieces of pine onto which have been glued pieces of strongly figured Honduras mahogany veneer, and there are two factors against this method of furniture construction. The first is that the ancient glue used will soften in either moisture or heat.

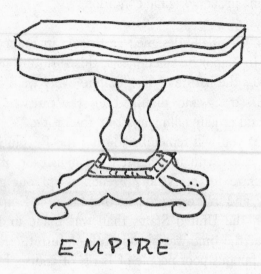

EMPIRE

Considering the furnitures of the kings who preceded him to be too effete, Napoleon adopted this style as being more expressive of his dreamed-of empire. But like his empire, it turns out to be mostly show. Although it looks solid, it actually consists of thin veneers of good Honduras mahogany glued onto bulky pieces of soft pine. As a result, the veneer is always chipping off as the pine under it shrinks in today's dry and overheated houses. Of course, it is dearly loved by those of us who make our living gluing back little pieces of veneer.

The second is that as it continues to dry out over the years the pine shrinks a little bit more than the mahogany veneer does.

The result of these two factors is a lot of corner chipping of the veneer on the edges of tops and drawers. As the pine base shrinks, the veneer begins to protrude so that it is easily caught and pulled away. This makes prevention, when still possible, easy. You just sand off the projecting lip of veneer with garnet paper wrapped around a square stick of wood.

When good size areas of the veneer are flapping in the wind, they can be ironed down due to the fact that the glue melts at fairly low temperatures. Set your iron for nylon, and experiment with raising the heat. To keep your iron from sticking to the shellac finish that is undoubtedly on the face of the veneer, cover it with waxed paper before ironing. If the piece is very dry, spray just a mist of water under the flap with an atomizer before ironing.

The patching of this veneer is easily done with Patching Sticks because the veneer is so dark. For using Patching Sticks see the introductory part of this chapter. You can also steal small pieces from the side, say, of a chest and use them to repair chipped places. For the technique used in doing this see the entry near the end of this chapter, *Veneered Pieces* (& Inlays).

If you have any Empire to sell, it is completely unappreciated in New England, and not much anywhere else *except* in the deep south where people are just wild about it for some odd cultural reason.

In fact it is so little valued in New England that the pine nuts up there strip the veneer off it, finish the revealed pine and try to pass it off to the unknowing as Early American pine. Which I suppose it is, when you think about it, except that it really isn't anything. Maybe the best term for it would be Naked Empire.

English Classic. This includes all the famous styles of the 18th Century—from Queen Anne through Chippendale, Hepplewhite, Adams and all the rest up to Sheraton. And the reason we can lump them together so outrageously is that they were all made about the same way with the same kind of tools, woods and glues. It was not only the greatest century of the British Empire (which is to say England, which is to say London) but it was the last century of the world before power tools and the resulting mass production came into being.

All these styles are still being made. Some in factories specializing in reproductions and plainly advertising their product as such. They are also being made by hand in a few hundred shops in England to supply the ever-growing market for fakes. To satisfy the English law or somebody over there they are gently labeled to be reproductions, but these labels fall off pretty soon, and if they are burned in they are burned in so shallowly that they

CHIPPENDALE

If the 1700's really are the Golden Century of Furniture design, it is because of the honest craftsmanship of the English cabinetmakers who were turning out Chippendale and the styles that followed for the rich merchant class that grew up with the expansion of the British empire. For the first time furniture was being mass produced for the solid people who like their furniture built solid and to last. And since it has already well outlasted the British Empire, they certainly got what they wanted.

are pretty soon sanded off as they pass from devious hand to devious hand.

The factory reproductions are easy to spot even if their exterior has been carefully distressed so that they look exactly like the originals from outside. Because their interior construction methods are unashamedly factory-made. Dowels are used instead of mortise and tenon joints. Drawer fronts are plainly attached to their sides by means of an obvious machine regularity and precision. Screw tightening braces are used for leg tops under the seats of chairs. Circular saw marks. No evidence of planing on backs of drawers—or bottoms. Perfect machine fitting everywhere.

But the fakes are something else again. They are made from patterns made from dissembled real pieces. Then the insides are aged by first a mild bath of lye water, then lightly stained. Even old-fashioned glues are used, and the outsides distressed with great care to duplicate marks and wear that have been carefully noted on museum pieces. Pieces of inlay are pried out and glued back in again. Inlays are carefully scratched between the little pieces of wood to make them look hand-cut. Original labels are reproduced, signed with brown ink, aged in mild solutions of muriatic acid (hydrochloric), stained and bleached and fastened on with rusty hand-cut tacks. Et cetera and inexhaustibly. And some of these pieces are already well over a hundred years old on their own.

Which is, of course, fraud, but it's such a nice old

fraud, and when you think of all the trouble these dear old duffers have gone to—and the excellence of the results—well, maybe they are worth as much as the real thing. At any rate, what would happen to the English economy if we stopped believing that Chippendale furniture can multiply like amoebae? Which must be the case because back in 1927 alone more of it was imported to this country than Chippendale could have made in his lifetime. Or at least it was so reported in a wonderful old book on this subject printed around that time and called "Goodby, Mr. Chippendale."

As to the restoration of such furniture, regardless of its true age, it was all beautifully fitted together of good cabinet woods (mostly real mahogany) that were well cured and have very little tendency to shrink. The finish invariably was—and still is—shellac, those nice old English fakers being sticklers for detail. And I must say that it is a delight to work on well-built stuff like this. And since five or six container loads of it are still arriving every week from England it looks like I'll never run out of the opportunity. So I say "Welcome, Mr. Chippendale!"

Fancy Chairs. These date from the 1830's and were originally sold around the country by peddlers, later by catalogue houses like Sears & Roebuck Co. Like Currier & Ives engraving they were among the earliest benefits to the common man of factory production, the very first beginning of our present society in which people aren't citizens any more but consumers. But they were still hand-decorated so I suppose that gives them some claim to being truly antique. And now that golden oak is commonly considered antique I suppose we have to call these chairs "early machine-made" antiques. Ah, where will it all end?

From the purist's point of view the objective is to preserve as much of the original decoration as possible. But this doesn't stop legions of ladies from completely redecorating them—along with tin trays and boxes. There may also be something of interest to you in the entry on *Hitchcock Chairs,* which follows in this chapter.

French Classic. While the English were having their Golden Age of Furniture Design the French across the channel were doing the same thing in making their Provencal and Louis 14th and 15th stuff—up to their revolution, of course, after which Empire came on the market.

But while this was as finely made as the English styles, there wasn't nearly as much of it. This was because while in England the middle class was rapidly expanding with the business of trading around the world, just the opposite was happening in France as the kings got meaner and meaner and the revolution finally had to come.

In other words, while the English styles were being made for the growing middle class, the French furniture was being made for royalty. Which is why it is mostly more delicate and always much decorated with paint, inlays, marble and brass.

Nor have these styles ever been much to the American taste. In the beginning it was rejected as being the product of a degenerate monarch and anti-revolutionary. (In those days, remember, revolution was a lot more popular in this country than it is today.) And now, though appreciated artistically, I think there is a consensus that it is too delicate, almost effete, for the American way of life.

An outstanding exception to this are the lovely but sturdy Louis 14th arm chairs which as an occasional piece fit in with the classical English styles. Just as a lacquered Chinese tea chest does because of the historical association. The creation of the finish on these chairs is covered in the entry *Antiqued Opaque*.

These are mainly distributed through interior decorator's shops, and as far as their authenticity as antiques goes, they average to be about a year to eighteen months old. They only get that old because of the peculiar way in which they come into being. The carved wooden pieces are made in Italy because the labor is cheaper there. The pieces are then tied in bundles and shipped to wholesalers in New York City who assemble them. From there they go to a finisher who sprays them with

FRENCH CLASSIC

Meanwhile, over in France the style that is named for Louis XV flourished, and could be called the French answer to Chippendale. It was also built strong and well, and also has stood the test of time in both usage and design. The later styles became more flimsy as did the English styles after Chippendale (Hepplewhite, Adam, Sheraton, for instance).

white lacquer and antiques and distresses them. The interior decorator then gets ahold of them and either upholsters them himself or has them done by the decorator's shop.

Hitchcock Chairs. Made in a fair imitation of the lines of American Sheraton, these were the most widely distributed of the *Fancy Chairs;* see above. The ones now being made by the revived Hitchcock Company are easy to tell from the originals by the fact that they are made of sturdier sections and the turnings are not as fine. Also the decoration makes, to my eye at least, no attempt to resemble the original handwork of stenciling, hand-painted motifs and the characteristic carriage striping. On the originals the decoration on no two chairs was ever *exactly* alike. On the modern ones it is.

However fake hand-redecoration on original Hitchcock chairs is endemic, and when it has been executed by anyone with artistic ability equal to the original decorators, it is impossible to detect—short of chemical analysis of chips of the paint used, which isn't worth the expense.

It is hard to establish a point in their destruction where the restorer should try to preserve traces of original decoration. It simply depends on individual judgment and how much of a purist you are. Certainly when the old decoration is almost entirely worn off there is nothing unethical about replacing it, and that seems to

FANCY CHAIRS
(HITCHCOCK)

Fancy chairs were one of the first "luxuries" that the Industrial Revolution passed down to the common people. They were actually cheaply made and over-decorated versions of the Sheraton style that the rich folks liked at that time. And the peak of their mass-production came with the Hitchcock factory in the early 1800's. And because of the integrity of the Connecticut brothers Hitchcock they were the best made.

me to be the only sane course. The only problem is whether you want to label your work as a recreation or not, and these ethical questions are far beyond the grasp of my simple mind.

Victorian, walnut. Popular around and after the Civil War, this is well-built stuff of fine wood and seldom in need of repairs. The problems that come up usually concern the marble tops. For information concerning cleaning, cutting and shaping marble see the entry on *Marble Tops.*

Victorian, oak. After some early stumbling around when this first flooded the market everyone seems to have settled for removing the old varnish and then just soaking it with boiled linseed oil for a soft dull finish which on oak is very serviceable. Table tops that get a lot of use will appreciate another rub-down with oil once a year. I should add that there are many people who swear by mineral oil drained from the crankcase of their automobile. I'll admit that this looks as good, the smell just isn't as nice.

The tops of most oak tables were made of wide boards planked together, but some were made of fairly narrow boards planked together and then covered with sheets of oak veneer. When this starts coming loose due to being water soaked it also warps badly and is very hard to glue back down. You can't effectively clean the old glue out from under the veneer so that new glue will hold. And these tables aren't worth any more effort than that—still being worth only thirty-five dollars in the rough as this is written. So you often see table tops from which the veneer has been soaked or sanded. This exposes the oak planking underneath and even though you then have narrower planks, this does not seem to affect the value of the piece. I suppose some people just *like* narrower planks in their oak table tops, so just removing the veneer once it starts going seems to be the obvious course to take.

Windsor Chairs. There is a lovely book around about these which is called something like *400 Windsor Chairs.* Every one different, of course, and that is their charm as well as the story of their origin. They were made throughout the northeastern part of the United States during the whole Colonial period and for another fifty years after that by country cabinetmakers who were mostly and often exclusively chairmakers. Anyone could throw together a bench or a table out of planks, but chairs took a foot or water-powered lathe and drills. And in the cast of curved back Windsors a hickory-steamer and bending press. Of which more in a moment.

Basically the legs are of turned maple, the seats of thick single pieces of pine and the curved pieces of hickory. Spokes and plain rungs could be of maple, hickory or poplar or fruitwoods. One sign of authenticity

VICTORIAN OAK

Oak furniture is the first that was purely the result of technology. It came into being because somebody invented woodworking machinery that had sharp enough and strong enough blades to cut fast. And of course, oak makes incredibly strong and durable furniture. But a couple of hack philosophers named Morris and Eastlake soon got into the act to help fancy it up with ridiculous and extraneous decorations. They called themselves "arbitors of taste," and their "taste" is having a big revival these days. Which is just another sign of the imminent collapse of Western (so-called) Civilization.

VICTORIAN WALNUT

During the early years of the Victorian era there was popular interest in the romance of things Italian. It started first in England and then came over to the U.S. in what was then called the Renaissance style. As in this piece it featured curved mouldings, carved pulls and marble tops. But best of all, it was made of beautiful solid walnut, which means that all of these pieces will last forever.

in these chairs is that these spokes were not made on lathes but shaved—with a tool called a spoke-shaver, of course, and it is still available in good tool stores.

Which reminds me that while the making of these chairs died out *substantially* in the middle 1800's there were a few isolated shops that carried on the art or craft as a father-to-son operation. To my own knowledge there was at least one such shop still in operation as recently as 1950 in the depths of Connecticut. And my instinct tells me that there are probably such shops being re-established. If I weren't so damned old, I'd open one myself. If completely handmade in the original way, reproductions of these chairs would be worth easily three hundred dollars apiece even with my name and the date burned lightly in the bottom of the seat. And if someone would sand my brand out and pass off the chair for an antique—as I'm sure someone would—well, then, the sin would be his not mine and I'd still be safe to reap my rewards in heaven for all my suffering here on earth.

The special problems that the restoration of these chairs present are broken curved hickory sections, short legs and loose spokes.

When a break occurs in a curved back it will always be where a hole was drilled into it to receive the top of one of the spokes, and the only way to repair this is with a lapping patch about three inches long. As this is too hard to explain in words alone, see the accompanying illustration.

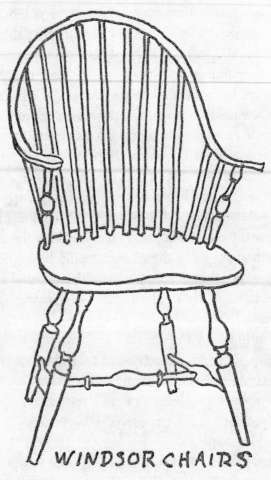

WINDSOR CHAIRS

There are very few ultimates in this life, but I don't think anybody in his right mind would argue with the contention that the Windsor chair is the finest thing that man has ever conceived and made out of wood.

The method used to lengthen legs a few inches is shown in the introduction to this chapter. This is a frequently needed repair—if you want to be able to sit in the chair with any dignity—because so many of these chairs started out their lives on dirt floors in taverns. The ultra-purist might not want to make this repair, but most serious antiquarians accept it as a necessary evil if the patch is left obvious by not staining the new wood to match the old.

Back spokes are easily and perhaps best (if they are not hickory) replaced by shaving down common dowels to match the other spokes. This dowel is poplar and will take stain nicely to give you an exact color match. And I for one see no point in leaving this kind of a repair unstained. It would be jarring to the eye as well as sort of pretentious or at least a piece of vulgar one-upsmanship.

A funny piece of trouble you will run into in replacing a spoke—or even trying to remove one for re-gluing—is that you will find you can't get the bottom of it out of its hole in the seat as loose as it may appear to be. My first experience with this almost drove me up a wall one day until my Uncle George or some other old faker explained to me that there was a ball on the end of the dowel, which had been popped into the hole with a mouth smaller than the ball.

This is fine if you like chairs that rattle, but for re-gluing there is no way to get this ball out so you can clean

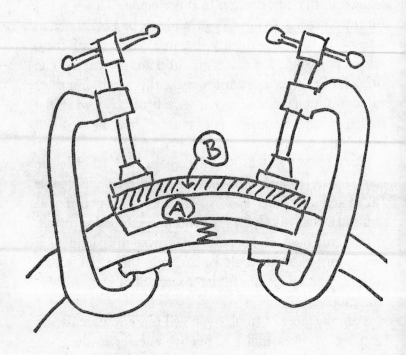

At this point in the process A and B are, of course, the same piece of wood. After the Glue has cured for forty-eight hours you can remove the clamps and shave off the shaded section of our patch (B). Such repairs to Windsor chairs are rarely camouflaged with stains or touch-up powders—I think because they make a chair look even more interesting.

out the old glue before re-gluing. Not without splintering the surface of the chair seat. So it's either a poor glue
job or a splintered chair seat, and the choice is yours.
How much splintering there will be if you pull the ball
out of its socket is impossible to predict, though naturally you can always glue it back down as carefully as
possible.

Bending hickory is the real hang-up in repairing or
reproducing Windsor chairs. Because in the first place
you don't want dried out wood, so you are going to have
to find your own hickory tree and cut it down, and of
course saplings are far the best for bending. Then you
want to split your strips out of a plank about forty inches
long. You can do some rough sawing, but splitting will
give you better continuous fibre which is less likely to
split in the bending process.

The steaming or boiling of these strips, which are not
left oversized at all, but planed down to exact size desired, is then easier than it looks, because all you need is
a stove-pipe a little longer than your sticks. You simply
solder tin on one end, and this gives you in essence the
tallest pot in the world. You put water in the bottom of
it, insert your stick, affix a cover and boil away for about
two days or longer. This is variable according to how hot
your steam is and the age of the wood. Saplings cut in
August are said to be best.

The wood is then slowly bent into shape and thoroughly dried. A whole winter in back of the stove is best. This bending is done with pegs on a board as illustrated, and you have to overbend about ten percent to account for a slight return. The less tension in the wood when you drill your holes to receive the tops of the spokes the better.

For each piece you want to make, I suggest you steam five. That's two for disasters in bending or drilling, one for your chair and two extras for future jobs. But store these spares in their bent position by tieing the ends together with string or they will gradually revert to almost straight.

There is of course another kind of Windsor chair that is smaller and contains no bent hickory. These are characterized by so-called "bamboo" turnings and sometimes birdcage backs. See illustration. In these the problems presented are not special—except that there are an amazing number of fakes around. This is mainly due to the fact that Francis Haggerty, the boss at Cohasset Colonials in Cohasset, Massachusetts, has been making such excellent reproductions of them for lo these many years. These get antiqued in a wild variety of ways, and about the only way you can tell them for sure is that the seats are planked up. And this is so often concealed by paint, stain, grime, shellac, varnish, touch-up powders that you have to sand across the bottom of their seats to find out.

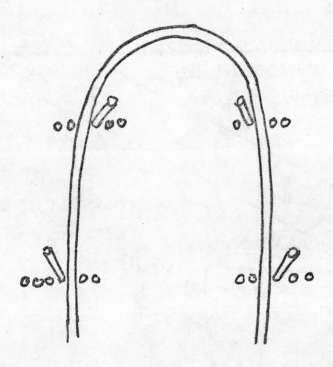

Bottom pegs are moved in gradually while hickory is wet
to establish the bend. This is done in about four hours.
Then hickory is allowed to dry out thoroughly. A couple
of weeks hanging behind a hot stove is about right. I
suppose that means it would take several months at
ordinary house temperature, but to tell the truth I can't
see anybody doing this unless he had a hot stove,
anyhow.

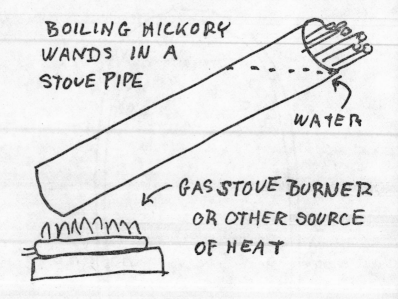

BOILING HICKORY
WANDS IN A
STOVE PIPE

WATER

GAS STOVE BURNER
OR OTHER SOURCE
OF HEAT

Don't worry if you have a high stove or a low ceiling.
Water will boil at an angle as well as it will straight up
and down. Actually stove pipe tin is too flimsy for this
kind of usage. What you really do is go down to your
local welder and have him make up a tube about four
feet long and ten inches in diameter out of galvanized
sheet metal. And be sure to have him put a bottom on it,
too.

The end of the line was reached a couple of years ago when a nice little old Yankee lady brought Mr. Haggerty an original to see if he wanted to buy it from her for his reference collection. Oldest looking thing you ever saw. But you guessed it—it was one of his own. Though he says he had to look it over for four or five minutes to be sure himself.

HARDWARE

There is a lot more hardware used in furniture than we ever think of—unless somebody has lost a piece. You can get all kinds of hinges, latches and locks, casters and feet from the mail-order catalogues listed in the Appendix, of course, but if you are looking for something really rare, I suggest you stop in and ask every antique dealer whose shop you pass. You'd be amazed at the collection of *junk* these people have in cardboard boxes in their back rooms.

KNOBS

For brass ones see under *Brasses* above. That leaves knobs of wood, porcelain and glass, and we will take up all three here.

The first thing you should know is that all dealers collect sets of these just as they do casters. They don't have them lying around out in their shops for sale, but they've got 'em. In ratty old shoe boxes in their back rooms, and for a reasonable return will sell them to you if you ask. And if you are only missing one knob, they will give you something for your five against the six they have that will make your piece a complete masterpiece.

Sets of glass and porcelain knobs are also advertised from time to time in *The Antique Trader*, as are lines of reproductions of knobs. Or if you run an ad telling what you want in that paper, you will get all kinds of replies.

Wooden knobs, of course can be duplicated from scratch. For a bunch of them you would need a lathe. But if you have the patience for this sort of thing, you will be amazed at what you can do whittling away at a piece of wood while you sit chatting with your family around the fireplace on a long winter evening. Holding your piece of wood against a disc or belt sander while you rotate it will work a lot faster, but these things are always a matter of taste.

LEATHER TOPS

These can be waxed. They can be stained with wood stains. They can be resurfaced by wiping their lacquer finish off with lacquer thinner, and then respraying them with a spray can of clear lacquer. Cigarette burns in them can be fixed with shellac sticks the same way you use them on wood. (See section on *Patching* in Part I.)

And best of all, leather tops can be replaced. The only trouble is that to find someone to sell you the leather you will have to go to some big city like Boston or Atlanta or Los Angeles, etc. Then you look in the "yellow pages" under "Leather," of course, and go the block they are all going to be located on.

Or you can let your interior decorator do all that for you. Or if you can make friends with an interior decorator, he will get it for you wholesale.

The leather comes already covered with lacquer, or you can easily spray it. And, naturally, you cut it to size with the most carefulness you can muster, using a steel straight edge and a fresh single-edged razor blade.

The gold decorations strips near the edges are stamped in a square at a time with gold leaf, and it is hard to find such a stamp, because for hand work and repairing leather artisans grind their own. However, for touch-up work good stationery stores sell sheets of "gold" leaf backed by clear plastic that you can press to lay gold onto almost any surface.

MARBLE TOPS

Let's face it at the beginning: stains in marble are hard to take out. This is because marble is not only

porous—like the finest kind of sponge—it is also translu-
cent. This means that stains can sink in deeply, and still
be seen even after they are removed from the surface.
They will show up through a bleached out surface. Of
course, the degree of this translucency varies—as does
the porosity—so some marbles respond to cleaning far
better than others.

So that being said, the technique is to make a poultice
to soak the marble with your stain-removing solution for
three or four days before you even look at it. This is
done by making a slurpy paste out of whiting—which is
powdered white chalk that you buy at any good paint
and hardware store—and whatever liquid you are hoping
will attack the stain. To keep this paste wet you can
cover it with plastic and check it out to see if it needs
more liquid once in a while. You can also use waxy modeling clay to build a retaining wall around your slurp so
that you can make it wetter.

Now it is usually hard to tell what made the stain, but
we can start with a process of elimination. If it is oily or
greasy looking what you need is acetone, a highly volatile thinner that is like lacquer thinner only more so.
Some paint stores have it, but all boatyards are a better
bet, because it is the thinner for the epoxy mixtures they
use to put glass cloth on the bottoms of boats with. Obviously because it evaporates so fast you will have to
refresh your slurp often with this.

The next most obvious thing is a rust spot, and you make your slurp with a widely available product called Naval Jelly, which will dull the surface of course, but we'll come to that in a minute.

Next most obvious is ink, and the solution is sodium hypochloride—which for anybody who doesn't know it yet is Clorox and similar liquid laundry bleaches.

The rest of the stains in their infinite variety can be attacked with hydrogen peroxide and a few drops of water the same way you would bleach your hair.

As to the dull area on your shiney marble top that you now hopefully have instead of the stain, this can only be restored by high-speed buffing with fine polishing compounds. In other words, you have to take your table to somebody who makes gravestones.

Not really. What you do is you dull the whole top with whatever you used on the spot. Then finish the surface with a thin coat of spray lacquer. Polish it with "ooo" steel wool and wax it.

MUSICAL INSTRUMENTS

Well, I've got a lot of nerve, and I expect you to have it, too, but I think that to presume to repair a fine antique violin or other wooden musical instrument once it has been bashed in would be going a little bit too far for

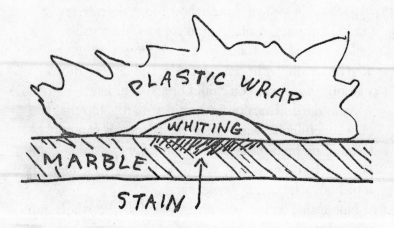

This is a cross-section of how you make your basic poultice for treating stains in marble tops. The way you preserve marble left out of doors for a few centuries is to paint it with hot beeswax dissolved in an equal amount of mineral spirits or turpentine. You only have to do it about once every fifty years.

both of us. Especially when there still are many crafts-men who devote their lives to making these things. I take any such problems of my own to Moe Van Dereck in Provincetown, Massachusetts. The way to find such a person in your own locality is through your local coffee house, because all the young guitar players know about such craftsmen. And if you are really serious, the best are reputedly in Barcelona, Spain. Except that the best of the best is the *Estudio de Jose Ramirez* up in Madrid.

However, if the problem is one of appearances, you can rest assured that the finish is a high grade of shellac that will respond completely to a light padding with lac-quer thinner. Or if the finish has been or has to be re-moved, it can be exactly replaced with French Polishing. For the correct method of applying a shellac finish see the introduction to the section covering finishing tech-niques.

PANELS

The inherent problem here is that panels split, and the reason is that by original intention they were sup-posed to float free inside of a frame. I mean, that's what a panel is by definition. Whether your panel is part of a library wall or the side of a chest of some sort. The point was to allow for expansion and contraction of a relatively wide piece of wood that would be subject to varying heat and moisture content in the air it was meant to live in.

So if your piece is going to be kept in a stable atmospheric condition it is all right to fill a crack in a panel however you see fit. But naturally the most correct approach is to free the panel scraping out whatever is making it stick to the vertical sides of its frame, glue it together, and allow it to remain "floating" in the future. Picky, picky work, but that's what this restoring business is all about.

PESTLES

Once a pestle splits all you can do is fill the crevice with a wedge of matching wood, and then touch up your repair with stain and touch-up powders. These won't take any wear, but then any pestle old and interesting enough to be worth repairing is too good to be using anyway.

SIGNS

For retouching the paint on old ones, see your local artist. As to replacing pieces of weathered wood, newly made pieces can be aged quickly by immersing them in strong baths of lye, Clorox and finally chlorinated lime, all of which are available at your friendly super market.

The lengths of time for each bath depend on the kind of wood, the temperature and the effect you want, so you have to experiment, but you can start out thinking in terms of about a half an hour for the lye and ten minutes each for the Clorox and lime.

SLEIGH SEATS

These are made into benches by building some kind of a box to go under them to raise them to a reasonable height for sitting on. Then they are usually painted a dull black, carriage striped on the back and base and given a colorful pillow seat. Personally I wouldn't have anything that quaint in my house, but then I'm working hard to build an international reputation as an antiques snob.

SPOOL TURNINGS

See first part of this book under the general subject of *Staining*. Replacements are obviously made on a lathe!

TABLES

My original files for this had the subject broken down into tables, round; tables, square; tables, pedestal; tables, stretcher . . . and so on into the night. But that was just

another example of my Germanic passion for over-or-
ganization getting out of hand again. My Irish common
sense, which I get from my mother's side of the family,
tells me that the basic problem with tables is common to
all of them. And that is that they get loose and start to
fall apart. And the solution in all cases is the same.

You don't just squirt some glue in the loose joints.
You take the whole thing apart, scrape out the old glue
and then glue it back together again using thin slivers of
wood to fill in loose places. Nor is this ever very difficult
once you take the time to turn your table upside down
on top of another table that has been covered with a
couple of layers of blanket. Then you knock it apart with
a padded hammer or rubber mallet or by cushioning
your hammer blows with small scraps of wood. Also see
directions at the beginning of this section about gluing
and other mysteries of woodworking such as curing
warped tops. The really troublesome problems we run
into with tables is in . . .

TABLES, DROP-LEAF

—And these troubles are all because of, or related to,
the hinges that support the leaves. Sometimes the screws
rust out and loosen. Then one end of the leaf drops
down and twists or breaks the hinge on the other end.
Or even worse, the top of the table shrinks to become

narrower than the frame it rests on so that when the leaves are lowered the screws are pulled out.

Let us get rid of the narrowing tops first. You could widen the top, of course, but that would be butchery. The only couth solution is to narrow the frame by taking it apart and shortening the end pieces before gluing everything back together again. See illustration.

The problems with hinges fall in three classes: torn out screws, bent hinges and broken hinges. So in that order, here goes.

Torn out screws: Unless they are terribly rusted, it is always best to retain the original screws. To begin with you can be sure they are the right length and won't go pushing through the top of your table on rescrewing. If you are replacing screws, just be very, very careful, which in most cases will mean grinding the point off your new screws.

If the wood fibres in the hole from which the screw has been torn is still strong, all you will need to reset the screw in the hole is to first wet the hole with a little Weldwood Plastic Resin Glue (see beginning of this section), then push a paste made of fine sawdust and the same glue into the hole. Replace your screw and let it dry before putting any stress on the hinge. (All this work is, of course, done with the table top upside down on your padded work table.)

In the case of real damage or punky wood, you may

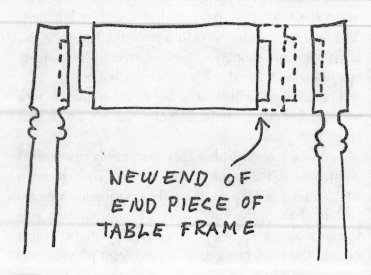

NEW END OF
END PIECE OF
TABLE FRAME

When the top of a drop-leaf table shrinks it either splits or pushes the leaves off their hinges when the leaves are lowered. The only real answer to this is to make the table frame narrower by shortening the end pieces. The tops of the legs will knock off the ends of the end piece quite easily, but I can't imagine trying to shorten the end piece without a table saw and some experience using one. And yet . . . in the olden times . . . !

want to drill out the holes with a quarter-inch drill and glue in pieces of quarter-inch dowels. Then you will later have to drill sixteenth-inch holes into these to get your new screws started. The way you stop yourself from drilling all the way through your table top with your quarter-inch drill is by putting a stop collar around it. You can get these in good tool stores or if necessary, you can make one out of wood as illustrated.

Bent hinges: These can usually be pounded back into shape cold, but it is worth the extra time to heat them with a blow torch or over a gas stove flame to be safe. Don't melt them, just get them good and hot. That's when the first glimmer of red begins to show on any edge.

Broken hinges: Table hinges are awfully hard to find in local hardware stores, because, I suppose, there is so little call for them. Sometimes you will find decorative brass hinges (or brass coated steel) that can be ground into shape. But the best thing to do is to order them from the *Constantine* catalogue. (See review of supply catalogues at the end of the book.)

(In case this sounds like I am making a mountain out of a molehill to you, the point is that table leaf hinges are different from regular hardware and even regular cabinet hinges in the holes for the screws that go into the leaf are—and have to be—further away from the pin than the holes for the screws that go into the center piece.)

UPHOLSTERED CHAIR FRAMES

As a mere humanist I cannot get involved in the philosophic question of when it is correct and when it isn't to replace the upholstery and how much of it on an antique upholstered chair. I leave all such judgments up to the experts of the world—interior decorators, museum directors, town managers, Jesuits and so forth.

But given that such a job has to be done, you will find that the original glue used has given up long ago, and your frame will become a veritable rattle as soon as it is no longer held together by the strings, webbing, padding and material of the upholstery.

If the frame is at all complicated you can make a drawing of it before knocking it apart, or number the pieces some way, to give you a clue to how it goes back together. For gluing instructions see the beginning of this section, but I will add here that when working on a chair or couch frame you can do an awful lot with tourniquets made of clothesline. Especially in tightening up round-backed chairs. Also, strap clamps are made for just this purpose, and can be had from the *Constantine* catalogue (see catalogue reviews at end of the book). And they sell pipe clamps, too, which are also useful for gluing up these frames.

Before delivering your frame to an upholsterer make

sure you gain his good will by cleaning it thoroughly with a damp cloth and removing all tacks and traces of previous padding, webbing and material. Also fill in any holes into which he will be tacking with Plastic Wood.

VENEERED PIECES (including Inlays)

The problems here fall in two divisions: 1) Reattaching loose or flapping pieces or pieces that have fallen off or out but that you still have, and 2) replacing broken off or fallen out pieces that have been lost.

For tacking down a flapping piece of veneer the basic thing you need to know is that the glue used for attaching veneer to all antique furniture—even up through the Golden Oak period of the early 1900's—was always an animal glue—hide, rabbit, hoof, fish, or whatever—and they are all the same in how they behave. With the right proportion of water in them they are hard at room temperature, but will melt when heated in a double boiler.

Now this quaint characteristic results in the odd fact that pieces of flapping or loose veneer can often be ironed back into the place with an ordinary hand iron set at "nylon" to start and pressing the veneer down through a couple of sheets of wax paper. You then have to either hold the iron in place while it cools, or arrange for some other way for the pressure to be maintained on

TOP OF TABLE

SCREW WITH POINT FILED OFF

HINGE

The best way to get a really fat screw to replace an old rusted out one—and thus get a grip in the old hole—is to grind or file the point off of a bigger screw. Of course, you clean out the hole well first, squirt in glue and stuff it with toothpicks when necessary. I don't want to hurt anybody's feelings, so I won't mention any names, but stuffing the hole with a wood filler—any wood filler—just doesn't do the job, because it doesn't penetrate into the wood around the hole the way glue does.

the veneer while the glue cools. Piles of encyclopedias, for instance. If this doesn't work the first time, what you need is more glue. You can order this under the name "Cabinet Flake Glue" from the *Constantine* catalogue. (See catalogue reviews at end of the book.)

You get your veneer loose again by reheating with the iron and gently prying the veneer loose again. Grind this flake glue into a fine powder and push it in where needed. When heated with your iron it will squish around inside quite satisfactorily. Squeeze out and scrape off any excess.

Pieces of inlay are just small pieces of veneer, so you can handle their refastening the same way. Or you can simply use any white glue as this will adhere well enough to the old original glue if you have scraped it clean of any grease, wax or dirt.

Now for replacing lost pieces of veneer or inlay there are some tricks that will make this a lot easier than it looks like it will be at first.

To begin with, you can get any kind of veneer from the *Constantine* catalogue. This includes holly which is the basic wood used for replacing lost pieces of inlay because it is fine and smoothgrained, almost white, and will stain to match anything quite beautifully—using any kind of stains, including water colors. From *Con-*

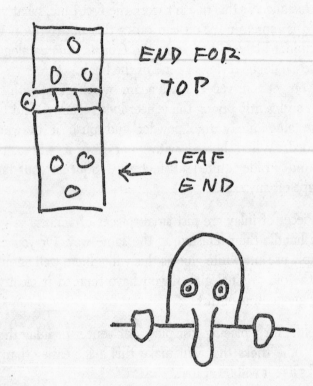

Hinges for table leaves are different because one end has
to be longer than the other. They have to be for the
leverage involved. It's hard to explain—just try an
even-ended one, and you'll see what I mean. And table
leaf hinges are hard to find in your friendly local
hardware store, too. See catalogues in appendix.

stantine you can also get strips of inlays, even chess boards and whole round table tops thirty inches wide. Even matched veneers for rectangular table tops and drawer fronts. These and many other wonders all come perfectly fitted and pasted to sheets of brown paper. And the idea is that you glue them wood side down to your base wood, then when your glue has set, you sand off the paper backing. That's *one* neat trick.

Another is that when you are replacing veneer with a fresh sheet of matching veneer you can stain and finish the new piece before you glue it on. Or five or six over-sized pieces of veneer until you get one just right, which is much better than messing around after the veneer patch is glued on.

The third trick that might not occur to you the first time you do this is that your patch piece doesn't have to conform to the shape of the piece that is missing. Your work will be neater and less noticeable if your patch is diamond shaped and the area that receives it has been trimmed to exactly fit your in-going diamond. There are die cuts for this sort of thing, but they are passed down from father to son. What you can do is make a diamond out of a piece of thin metal and cut both your patch and the new edges of your hole using it as a guide. Doing your cutting with a single-edged razor blade, of course. Or you can cut the new edges of the receiving hole at

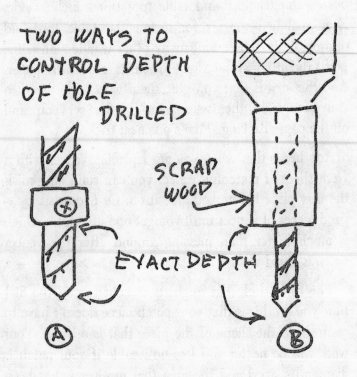

TWO WAYS TO
CONTROL DEPTH
OF HOLE
   DRILLED

SCRAP
WOOD

EXACT DEPTH

(A)   (B)

Whenever using dowels, it is often important not to drill
too deep. The steel drill collars in (A) are great, but
hard to find. The alternative is to make your own depth
stop by drilling through a piece of wood just long
enough to leave the desired length of drill point sticking
out. As in (B).

the same time you cut your patch by cutting it through the piece of veneer out of which you are cutting your patch.

Now doesn't that make it all sound easy? And it is—if you have always been the kind of person who is "good with his hands," or however the saying went on your block. But if you weren't . . . well, why don't you see if you can get your money back on this book?

And don't even think of trying the truly easiest way of restoring inlays and small chips of missing veneer around edges. Your professional restorer—or "polisher" as he is called in the trade—would invariably use shellac sticks to fill the holes, a little touch-up powder smudged on with his skillful fingertip and a final padding with lacquer—for all of which mysteries and magic see the first part of this book.

WICKER

You can really amaze yourself with the results you'll get restoring even the most decrepit pieces of old wicker furniture.

First you scrub it clean with soap and water, and then rinse it exceedingly well with a garden hose. This not only cleans it but puts moisture back into the reeds and cane so that it will once again stretch and bend without breaking.

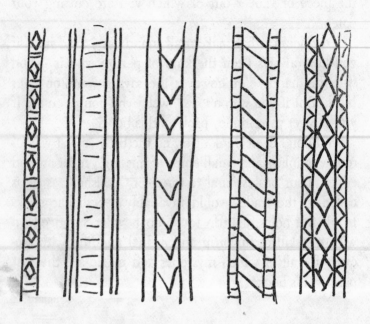

When little pieces of inlay stripping are missing from
your old Italian end table or reproduction Hepplewhite
sideboard, don't let it cause you a moment of insecurity
or anxiety. Constantine will take care of you. That's the
big mail-order house for everything that has anything to
do with wood. And in this case, they have a vast
assortment of inlay strips, shown in full color in their
catalogue. For more information see Appendix.

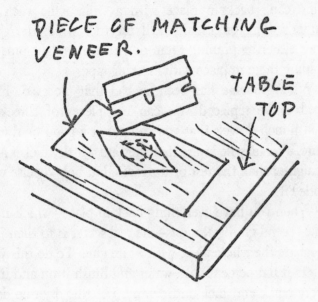

PIECE OF MATCHING VENEER.

TABLE TOP

This is how you get a veneer patch to be exactly the same size and shape as the hole it will be glued into. You simply cut the patch and the hole at the same time with a single-edged razor blade. What keeps your top piece from sliding around? Well if you are near the edge, you can use a "C" clamp. Inland you glue it down temporarily at the corners with rubber contact cement. Use according to instructions! Then after your cutting, the corners can be pried free with a pallet knife.

After the piece has dried overnight, you then tediously glue each broken reed or unraveled piece of covering cane back in place with a white glue such as Elmer's. The pieces are held together while the glue dries either by pinning them down with straight pins or holding them in place with masking tape.

When damage has been so bad that pieces of reed need to be replaced you can use pieces of three-sixteenth-inch dowels that you can get at a good hardware store. You may be aware that they are a little thicker and straighter than the rest of the reeds, but nobody else will notice it.

When you have everything back in place—which may take several gluing sessions—the real secret is to then impregnate the whole piece with white glue. To do this you dilute it ten percent with water and brush it on and into every crack and nick and cranny. Let this dry one day, and give it another coat of glue. Let this second coat dry for two days, and your piece is almost as strong as when it was new.

Incidentally, the reason for using a white glue instead of Weldwood powdered glue is that while Weldwood may be the strongest glue, it dries to a rigid state similar to cast iron. Thus as the wicker gives and moves—especially in a chair—the reeds and cane will break away from it. The white glues dry to a state of just enough pliability to give with the slight movement of the reeds.

ZATLINS

I'll bet you thought I'd never think of anything that began with a Z, didn't you? But I've got a lot of time. I thought of *Zeppelins* right away. But how often do you find a Zeppelin made out of wood? Of course, *zemis* are made out of wood, but how many of you are aborigines living in the West Indian islands?

For a while I considered *zigzag*—as in moulding on late Victorian oak furniture. And of course you often find a lot of wood in a *zeotrope*, which is of course, a mechanical toy consisting of a revolving cylinder in which the effect of motion is produced by pictures on the inner surface of successive positions of a moving object viewed through slits in the circumference.

And what would be the matter with a *zither* or a *zinke*? But I am a practical man, so it was easy for my wife to convince me that I should write about something beginning with a Z that most people have around their houses such as the ordinary, everyday *zebra wood zatlin* that we all know so well. And which gives us *two* Z's to boot!

So getting down to cases the problem with these pieces is that the warm, dry air we have in our houses in the winter time causes these pieces to fall apart. And just squirting glue into their slotted joints doesn't work.

The reason for this is that the zebra wood is so hard—and greasy from having been soaked in oil—that no glue will soak into its surface. That is why they were in fact never glued together in the first place, but were tightly fitted and jammed together.

Years ago I fixed a table like this for a man who had once been our American consul in Peking. He had collected a lot of antiques over there and had observed how the rich Chinese took care of the problem when it occurred in their well-heated embassies and so forth.

In brief, what you do is think of the damn stuff as metal, and drill holes in it and bolt it together. Honest. And it works. In most cases you will want to use washers, and lock nuts are *de rigueur*. Naturally you will want to countersink any bolt heads that show and fill the hole with the patching material of your choice or even a plug of wood cut from a dowel the same diameter as the countersink drill that you used. If any of the plug sticks up above the surface, trim it with a single-edged razor blade or a perfectly sharpened chisel. Then stain with a dark walnut alcohol-type stain so that it will get good and dark. If the plug goes in a little bit too far, I'd just leave it be (though stain it of course) and tell people that's an authentic sign of age.

Part III

More About My Infamous
Uncle George
(And My Aunt Mary, too!)

My Uncle George & the Artist Fellah

A very special kind of put-down that they are still talking about in old Bath, Maine.

People are always asking me if my Uncle George is real, or I just made him up. Of course, he's real. Or was. We buried him six years ago this coming April. Had to. He was dead. He never intended to die, but at ninety-three he was ripe for it, so one morning he just didn't wake up.

I was pretty shaken up by it at the time, but as the years go by the pain of his loss has faded and he sort of reassembles himself in my mind. The good memories come back and fit themselves together, and he is real and whole again, at least in my mind.

For those of you who never heard of him before, my Uncle George was an old Yankee cabinetmaker up in Vermont who used to let me help him in his shop when I was a boy. He was a kind man and funny as hell, but being a Yankee he'd rarely let you catch him smiling.

Maybe when he was alone he'd let himself smile, but I never found out.

Of course, I could talk about him from now to doomsday and never get across to you what he was like as well as I can do it by telling you just one little thing that he did. For instance, he used to tell me with relish about a good one he got off back when he was only a boy of twenty-one.

At the time he was working in a big hardware store down in Bath. That's a town on the coast of Maine, and about the most exotic place he ever traveled to outside of Vermont. But he was sowing his wild oats and seeing the world while he was young, he used to say. "Ayup," he used to nod with satisfaction, "I seen the ocean." He was mocking himself and all Vermonters, of course, but if you didn't understand that, he wasn't about to explain it to you.

But getting back to the hardware store, he was clerking there, and one fine summer day he got a call from that artist fellow from New York City that had bought the Perkins place up on Roast Meat Hill. (The origin of that name goes back to a day in the early 1800's when a half a dozen or so cows got killed in a forest fire.)

Anyway, the artist fellow was doing some remodeling on the place, and he had called in to place a long order of materials he wanted delivered up there. So he was reading off the items he wanted from his list kind of fast, and my Uncle George was trying to catch up. So after a while the artist fellow paused, and when he didn't hear anything from my Uncle George for what seemed to him a long time he said into the telephone, "Are you still there?"

And since the man's impatience seemed unreasonable to my Uncle George he let about two seconds pass and replied, "Ayup—I just write quiet."

When my Uncle George was finished telling the story, he'd move his mouth around and kind of halfway grimace to keep from smiling and say, "Pretty good one, wahn't it, considering I was just a boy of twenty-two." And somehow I always thought that was the story he wanted to smile at the most. If it wahn't against the rules.

My Uncle George & Sartre & Camus & All Them

He used to say, "You can send a boy to college, but you can't make him think!"

During my high school years the school bus used to drop me off at about three in the afternoon, and my Uncle George would let me help him in his shop, which was right next to our house, until it was supper time. I was pretty full of myself in those days and I really took to "book learning," as we called it south of Rutland. (Which is a longer way than it looks from north of Boston!) So naturally I'd bait him once in a while, and one afternoon I asked him if he knew how they build the Pyramids. He was concentrating on fitting some joint together at the time, but he read me and what I was doing, and he answered clean as a whistle, "With a government grant, of course." No smile. And his eyes never left his work. But when he was done doing whatever it was he was doing, he turned to me and said, "All right, smart

aleck, now tell me how *did* they build the Pyramids?"
And he allowed himself about five percent of a smile to
show me there were no hard feelings.

Those were the good old days if only I'd known it,
though I do now. Later on, when I went off to college, I
think my Uncle George began to get jealous, because I
was getting more education than he'd ever had. Or
"schooling," as he would have called it to distinguish it
from learning about life from going through the living
of it.

Of course I came home for vacations and lots of week-
ends. Except in my senior year when I had personally
rediscovered the long known fact that girls are soft. And
that struck me as being as remarkable as the things you
can do with shellac sticks. But there I go trying to be as
funny as my Uncle George again, and I can feel his
ghostly presence standing behind me and muttering
"Still a little smart aleck, ain't-cha? If you'd stop laughing so hard at your own jokes you might be able to get
off a really good one now and then."

Anyway, getting back to my going to college, whenever I did get home I'd wander into his shop in the after-
noons just as I used to when I'd been just a kid in high
school and we'd talk a lot about life—sort of man-to-
man now that I was a grown-up. And of course whenever I'd learned any new words or ideas I'd drop them
very casually into the conversation. Real *suave*, that was
me.

One fall everybody on campus was reading Sartre and Camus and other existentialist writers. So when I came home for Christmas vacation I told him that I'd decided to become an existentialist. He snorted and said, "What the hell is that?"

So I explained to him how some French writers had developed this new philosophy that says that each man exists all alone in the universe.

He snorted again, and said, "Hell, everybody in Vermont knows that. Even the Indians. Where've these Frenchmen been all these years?"

"Well, it's more than that," I said. "It means that man didn't come from anyplace and isn't going anyplace. That there isn't any heaven or hell and life is meaningless." I realized even then that that was a pretty big ball to throw out at my Uncle George, him being a regular churchgoer even if he didn't do any whooping and hollering about it.

He looked at me with wonder in his eyes and said, "You mean to tell me they just found out about atheism over in France?" He paused a second and added, "And they think they *invented* it?"

I felt pretty put down, of course. Then. But as the years have rolled by I've come to realize that that was the beginning of my finally understanding that "book larnin" may be useful in life, but it doesn't hold a candle to learning to think for yourself.

My Uncle George's Favorite Joke

If you don't laugh, don't feel bad. You're o.k. It's the joke that's the matter.

The kind of jokes my Uncle George used to tell sometimes got so dry you could hardly believe they were even supposed to be funny. I think this is because they were far more than jokes—they were an expression of a philosophy of life. An attitude towards living and dying that is peculiar to what we would now call the Yankee experience. Meaning, of course, those long, hard and lonely winters—with each family isolated on its own farm, totally self-dependent. This making them fiercely independent—as in revolution. As in the first *successful* revolution in the history of the world. And against the most powerful nation of its time at that.

Now here's a sample, possibly one of the weirdest jokes ever told. And I want to warn you not to be expecting to laugh at the end of. No normal person would think it was funny. Only a Yankee. In fact, I hate to do this to you, but here goes.

It seems that two old cronies were sitting at the bar in a local tavern over in Poultney one afternoon. It was kind of quiet. Not much conversation going on. A lot of musing.

Both men were in their forties. Both of them had farmed and worked winters in the quarries all their lives. They were the real Vermont, alright. Winter in the quarries isn't bad because there isn't any wind down there and the companies have a humanitarian policy of stopping work whenever the temperature goes below minus twenty degrees.

Anyway, one of these fellows was named Huck and the other Remington. Huck is the one who is getting this good one off, which is to say pulling the other fellow's leg, so he speaks first, and the action goes like this:

Huck looks up from his beer to the calendar hung on the back bar. He looks at it for a long time. Then he looks down into his beer again and says, "Where were you this time last year, Rem?"

Remington turns his head to look at Huck and says, "Why I don't know. Here. I live here. Do you think I go to Florida for the winter?"

"No," says Huck, dragging it out, "I mean this day last year."

Remington takes a quick look at Huck and then looks

up at the calendar. After a while he says, "Ayuh, I see what you mean. It's Columbus Day, ain't it?" So he thinks about that for a long time, sorting out the events of the last year in his head.

Finally he says, "Now I remember. I went up to my sister's place to help my brother-in-law kill a pig."

"Too bad," says Huck. "If you'd been here you could have gone down to Rutland with us. We had a hell of a time. Ate in a Chinese restaurant and everything."

And that's it. That's the joke. It's all over. And I'm glad I didn't have to tell it to you face to face.

But you read it over a few times, and think about it. Not as a joke, but as a way of facing life. You see, what the Yankee has, that most Americans don't—at least these days—is a sense of the limits of our lives, no matter how well off or poor we are, or what we do for a living, or where we live.

It makes for a sense of the ridiculous. A gentle one. For Huck was making fun of himself, and all of us who take life seriously—not Remington. Real Yankee jokes are never on somebody else. They're just on being alive. Especially on being alive in Vermont, which is unquestionably ridiculous.

Variation on the Theme

I ought to be ashamed of myself for this. Skip it.

One day my Uncle George looked up at me from his workbench and said, "You know the most important thing about a good loser?"

I said, "No. What?"

He said, "He's a loser."

I let that sit for awhile. I was waiting for some explanation of why he happened to be thinking about the subject. I knew I wasn't supposed to ask any questions. That would be considered prying. The way city people do. In their barely forgivable ignorance. So I let it sit all afternoon, but he never said another thing. Nor ever again. I guess he forgot about it. Or maybe he just changed his mind.

Ayup, I sure wonder what he was thinking about that afternoon. If he'd told me, I bet it would have been real interesting.

If any of you out there are wondering why the hell I bothered to tell you this, it's just a little variation on the "good one" Huck got off on Remington a few pages back, and I thought I'd try my hand at it. If you don't think this one is funny either, I'm sorry. I guess you just don't have a good sense of humor, do yah? Leastwise, not in Vermont, you don't.

Of course, I don't mean any offense by that. I guess what I'm trying to say is that what you think is funny depends on who you are. And who you are depends on where you are—or where you came from. Where you grew up.

But I still think that if you didn't grow up in Vermont, you sure missed something rare. Take the time my Uncle George tried to get Mark Robinson to put in an upstairs toilet for him . . .

How to Speak Vermont

Or, the gentle art of buying something in a Yankee hardware store.

A lot of people go to Vermont, and don't like it. They think the people are unfriendly or at least unresponsive. And I'm sure it's true. But that's because most visitors don't know how to converse in Vermontese. It sounds like you're both speaking the same language, but you're not really. You're both speaking English words alright, but the difference is in the way they are put together— and the timing. Especially the timing.

I can do it. Sometimes without even thinking about it. But I'm usually conscious of doing it, because I had to learn. You see, I didn't go to live with my Uncle George until I was twelve. I had grown up in a big city, and spoke the usual American. Mostly by example. And a little nudge now and then to tell me to pay attention.

Anyway the way it goes is this. I'll use the situation of your going into a hardware store to buy something that isn't just lying around on a counter. Say, a leather valve for a hand pump. But what goes on would apply to going into a real estate office, a garage, any situation where you are making a first contact.

When you walk in they're pretty obvious about not looking at you, because they're sizing you up—to see if you are really one of them in spite of those funny looking city clothes you're wearing. Who knows, you might be Grant Everett's boy or some other smart aleck kid that left town after high school and thought he was too good to ever come back for a visit.

Now the first thing is you're not supposed to say anything like pushy city people do. And for God's sake, don't interrupt the fellow putting boxes of nails up on the shelves. Because if you do, he'll stop and wait on you alright, but he'll know you're an outsider. So he'll get you what you want, but he won't volunteer any information. Such as the odd fact that the nuts you picked out of the box don't happen to fit the bolts you picked out of the same box. After all, they were right in front of you, and all you had to do was look and see for yourself. How's he to know, maybe you have a special situation at home that calls for nuts that size and another one that needs bolts the other size. It isn't any of his business.

On the other hand, if you just stand there looking around the counters like you had all day—waiting for him to speak first—you'll have captured his attention, and he'll be able to think of you as another human being like him.

Now the second step is equally vital: You don't tell him what you want. What you do is say something foolish about the weather. If it's summer, you might say "Nice day." If there's a blizzard outside, try the same. This will intrigue him a mite, and he'll be listening to you, which is rare for a Yankee, and when he is most vulnerable. So sock it to him by asking him, "Lived here all your life?"

Now what this does is it gives him the *opportunity* to drawl, "Nope—not yet." And the thing is that he *knows* that you're giving him that opportunity, and to his strange mind that means that you are declaring you have come in friendship. You're not a threat to him, and you're not going to holler a lot of mean words at him if he is a mite slow about something.

Of course, he'll probably pass up the opportunity, and looking right in your eyes say a long "Hmmmmmmmmm," and then add, "What was it you were looking for?" Just why he will slip into the past tense like this is a mystery I have yet to fathom, but anyway, you are off and running with him when he does it.

Or going back a ways, he might speak first, and say to you, "Nice day." Or even a sloppy, "Nice day, ahun't it?" Now in this event, what is going on is that he's giving *you* the opportunity to say something like, "Well,

I'm feeling a mite sickly, but there's a lot of dead people who'd like it." That might be best, but if you're feeling a little feisty yourself, you might just look him straight in the eye and drop a long "Hmmmmmmm." And then add, "Well, I guess I need a few bolts—with nuts that fit on them."

My Uncle George & Robert Frost

That poem about mending walls is the one that stuck in his craw.

Of course my Uncle George never met Robert Frost, who was a famous poet, but then on the other hand, Robert Frost never met my Uncle George either. What happened was that when I went up to the University I discovered Frost's book of poems called "North of Boston." And since this was poetry about northern New England that was kind of a thrill. And on top of that it was poetry you could read. Writ in plain English, by gosh. With regular words that anybody could understand.

So naturally I brought this great find home with me one weekend to show my Uncle George. I think it was the long Thanksgiving weekend, and the idea was that that would give him the weeks until I came home again for Christmas to read it.

Well, that's what happened, alright, but the funny thing was that it turned out my Uncle George didn't think much of Robert Frost. The first problem was that it said right there on the book jacket that Frost came from over in New Hampshire, and that was suspicious right there. And then it told how he started out being a school teacher but now he was neglecting his work to write books on the side. "You'd think one trade would be enough for a man," my Uncle George mused darkly. "Hard enough to get to be an expert in one," he added with a warning look at me.

But what really stuck in my Uncle George's craw was the first poem in the book about mending stone walls. I suppose everybody knows the poem by now—this was years ago before Frost became as famous as he was in his later years. But the point of the poem is that in it Frost questions his neighbor's faith in the old saying that good fences make good neighbors.

"Well, damn," he'd half shout and pound the table, "of course good walls make good neighbors. And not just where there's cows like he says. It shows you got respect for other people's limits. In life, too, not just in fields. People have to have their lines drawn neat and clear between them or you'll have all kinds of trouble. And when you mend your walls with your neighbors it shows you got some respect for him and yourself, too." Then after a few grumbles he'd add, "Besides a messy wall looks like hell."

Well, I thought of all this the other day when I saw in a review of a book about Frost's letters how it has been coming out through the publication of those letters what a terribly unhappy family life Robert Frost really had. And I can't help thinking that maybe it is too bad Robert Frost didn't meet my Uncle George. Maybe my Uncle George could have taught him something about fences.

But on the other hand I've noticed that happy people don't write poetry very much. And for "two roads diverged in a yellow wood" someone had to pay the price.

My Aunt Mary's Telegram to Chicago

She could get off a good one herself—when she felt like it.

A lot of people have asked me about my Uncle George's wife—or if he even had one since I never mention her. Well, he did. And her name was Mary. But she was a strange one. She looked alright, just a nice little old farm lady, but she wasn't much of a communicator. As opposed to my Uncle George and me, of course, who talked all the time we were awake.

I remember that when I first arrived to live with them as a boy, for the first three days I thought she couldn't talk at all. Then I happened to see her down at the store chattering away like a bird with some other woman. And then it gradually dawned on me that her thing was that she just didn't talk to men. Unless it was absolutely necessary, and it was amazing how little she found it necessary.

And I never found out why. My Uncle George wouldn't talk about it. When I brought the subject up, he'd make believe he didn't understand me and there wasn't anything the matter. So I might as well have been talking to a tree. So I got the message and quit asking pretty fast.

She wasn't bitter. Or mean. She was always cooking good things and taking care of people. Including me. And him.

They went up the stairs and slept in the same room. I know that. And in the same bed, too, because I looked to see, and there was only one bed in the room.

And the funniest part of it all, to me, is that she used to get off a good one herself once in a while.

A real classic—and of course I heard about this some years after it had happened, but up in Vermont they remember the good ones a long time—was the time she sent her brother the telegram in Chicago.

It seems that her brother had run away from home to be an actor. And to her family this was such a degenerate offense that while they wouldn't admit that they thought of him as dead, they did. And my Aunt Mary was the only one who kept in touch with him. Well this time she got a letter from him just about two days before Christmas, and he told her how he was touring with some play, and they were out in Chicago and how lonely he was since he was the only single person in the company and the other actors didn't like him and so forth, and he ended up with how he wished he had taken the other road in the yellow wood so he could be home for Christmas.

Well, my Aunt Mary got worrying about that and feeling terrible for him. And then with a wild surmise she thought of sending him a telegram. And it was a pretty unusual idea, alright, because nobody in East Punket (Pop. 850 or so) had ever sent a telegram before. In fact, there wasn't even a telegraph office in East Punket at the time. You had to go down to Rutland to send one.

So she scrambled around and got a ride with somebody even though it was the day of her Aunt Emma's funeral and there weren't many buggies free in town. It must have taken all day. It was a good twelve miles and some pretty poor going to Rutland. But she got there and found the telegraph office down at the railroad station.

So the operator gave her the form, and she wrote down the message she had figured out on the way into the city. It wasn't the exact truth, but her heart was in the right place so she wrote down.

MERRY CHRISTMAS
FROM EVERYBODY. MARY.

Well the operator looked at that and counted the words and told her that it was only five and she could have ten for the same price. So my Aunt Mary took the form and the pencil back and thought for awhile and then added her five free words so that the complete telegram read as follows:

MERRY CHRISTMAS FROM
EVERYBODY EXCEPT AUNT EMMA.
SHE DIED TUESDAY. MARY.

Ayup. They still tell that one up in East Punket once in awhile. On those rare occasions when a stranger happens to wander into town.

My Aunt Mary's Pants

Or, having a good time in Rutland

I've got another one about my Aunt Mary, if you want to hear it. It's another strange one, and it's hard to tell whether she knew she was being funny or not. Like the story about the telegram she sent to her brother in Chicago. I'll admit that at first glance it looks like she is being funny without knowing she is. But it's awful hard to tell with Vermonters. And if they can make you think that they don't know they are getting off a good one, well that's the best kind of all.

Like the telegram story, this one also took place down in the big city of Rutland. Rutland seemed to bring out the best in my Aunt Mary. But it was quite a few years later because by then she and my Uncle George were married, and they owned a Model T.

Well, the core of the matter was that she and my

Uncle George had been down to Rutland a couple of months before on a regular shopping trip, and she'd bought three pairs of pants at the big department store there and when she got them home and tried them on they didn't fit.

She was talking to my Uncle George more in those days, and he told me that when she told him what had happened and how she had to make an exchange she lowered her voice whenever she came to the word "pants."

So they got there, and my Uncle George found a parking place very close to the front door of the department store. Since that was the only business she had in that store on this day, my Uncle George had agreed to sit there and wait for her. So she got out of the car and promising him she'd only be a few minutes she disappeared through the big glass doors and into the store.

Well, you know what happened. He waited fifteen minutes and thirty minutes, and started getting mad, and then telling himself he shouldn't get mad and finally began worrying about her. Maybe she'd fainted. Or met with foul play. A lot of strangers were coming into Rutland these days.

But after a whole full hour she finally showed up, and he was so relieved to see her that he didn't say a word about her causing him such an upset. And she was pretty flustered, too, and she had a tale to tell.

It seemed that the particular kind of pants she had

selected had wrong size markings on them, and half of them had the markings torn off by the salesgirls because they were wrong. And she couldn't find her size, so she finally borrowed a tape measure from one of the girls, a fine one, and went in the dressing room and measured herself to be sure she was the size she thought she was. Then she went back and started measuring the pants on the counter, and never did find a size better than the ones she had brought back with her.

So while she was telling my Uncle George all this she sat there in the car with the crumpled store bag with the original three pairs of pants in it. And when she was done, she just sat there for a while, and then began smiling. Finally she started chuckling out loud, and my Uncle George asked her, "What are you laughing at?"

Still smiling she turned to look at him and said, "But I got even with 'em!" And then she pulled it out of her pocketbook and showed him, "I stole their tape measure!"

And after he had told the story my Uncle George would say, "Now can you imagine a man doing a thing like that? I tell you, boy, women are strange." And he'd just shake his head in disbelief.

Appendix

Periodicals

THE ANTIQUE TRADER—Dubuque, Iowa 52001

This is a weekly, tabloid-sized newspaper, pushing towards
a hundred pages an issue and it's the only journal of the
antiques world that I subscribe to. Not that the others don't
have their value and uses to other people. But this paper
is particularly interesting to me as a restorer because of the
advertisements that run in it—for all kinds of materials,
parts, kits and how-to-do-it books and pamphlets.

It also has good articles about antiques and thousands of
listings of stuff for sale in its classified columns. It also
lists all the antique shows, and all the big dealers that sell
at wholesale prices to the little dealers also advertise in it.
(Incidentally, these wholesale dealers will sell to anybody,
even if you don't have a shop. But you have to show up
with a station wagon so have enough money with you to
fill it up. Do fill it at least halfway up, and *don't* quibble
about prices. If you do, the man there won't want anything

to do with you, and I don't blame him. He's running a legitimate wholesale business, and not a junkyard for cheap bargain hunters. Not that it isn't fun to be a cheap bargain hunter sometimes, but a wholesale dealer's barn isn't the place to do it in.)

HOBBIES—1006 South Michigan Avenue, Chicago, Illinois 60605

This is the magazine that almost all dealers subscribe to. It has been tops in the field for years and probably always will be. It's thick and packed full of ads listing thousands and thousands of antiques that dealers spend their lives buying from each other. Not as strong on crafts as I like, but you can find out the cost of almost anything by looking through the ads. In addition to furniture, finished and un-, it covers buttons, bottles, dolls, glass, china, stamps, books, coins, prints, firearms, Indian stuff, gems, postcards and like the fella says, lots, lots more.

Mail Order Catalogues

BOOKS

Mid-America Book Company, Inc.—Leon, Iowa 50144

This is the largest mail-order supplier of books on antiques in the country. They stock around 2,000 titles, and will probably find anything else in print that anybody asks for. This includes many how-to-do-it books. Good, fast, honest service, and as far as I can see the catalogue is free. Just ask for it, and tell the boss, John Brown, that I sent you.

Hotchkiss House—18 Hearthstone Road, Pittsford, New York 14534

Well, maybe these people think they have the biggest mail-order bookstore in the world. They have 1,400 titles on 60 kinds of antiques, a nice catalogue and they ship fast. And I see that my catalogue is a couple of years old, so maybe by now they have more titles than Mid-America. I better just sign off about now with the remark that both these houses put out fascinating catalogues and are fine to do business with.

BRASSES

HORTON BRASSES—Berlin, Connecticut

Send 50¢ for catalogue.

This is a complete line of classic brasses not cast, but struck from steel dies, so that they are exact reproductions. Even the nuts that attach the drawer face plates are cast of brass in irregular old molds and then tapped. A complete line for the classic English and Early American furniture styles—and now some of the better Victorian pulls and knobs.

CANING SUPPLIES

H. H. PERKINS Co.—10 South Bradley Road, Woodbridge, Connecticut 06525

This fine old family firm supplies a complete line of supplies for making cane and rush seats accompanied by very good (and free) illustrated instructions. And once you've started buying from them they will even help you with special problems that you run into. Providing you send in sketches, state your problem clearly and leave space for them to write in their reply. Send 25¢ for catalogue.

They also have supplies and instructions for basket weaving—with reeds. But that will cost you another quarter. After all, they're not in business only for the fun of it.

CLOCKS

Mason & Sullivan Co.—39 Blossom Ave., Osterville,
   Mass. 02655

One of those real old New England companies that carry
everything in their line and take care of their customers.
They have all kinds of kits to make fine big and little
clocks that are faithful reproductions of antiques such as
grandfather, steeple, wall and banjo cases. Also all kinds of
movements, barometers, thermometers, music box movements and even just plain good wood.

DECORATION SUPPLIES

Carson & Ellis, Inc.—1153 Warwick Avenue, Warwick,
   Rhode Island 02888

This is for the kind of people who paint pictures on tin
boxes and trays and the backs of Hitchcock chairs. Not
exactly my cup of tea, but they sure got the stuff from
brushes to patterns. They even sell lots of small tin things
and wooden boxes to use their paints on.

FINISHING SUPPLIES

Albert Constantine & Son, Inc.—2050 Eastchester Road,
   Bronx, New York 10461

Send 50¢ for catalogue.

A very old family firm that has been importing fine
woods and veneers since 1812, it is now a very modern and

efficient operation supplying everything it can think of for woodworking. All kinds of cabinet woods, veneers, preassembled inlays, trims, even guitar and clock kits. All kinds of hardware and hand tools, stains and finishes that can't be beat, lamp parts, cane, upholstery tools—everything for the cabinetmaker, with plenty of instructions, explanations and books on the many woodworking crafts involved. If you are less than a professional finisher, you can't afford to be without their "Constant-Stains." These come in all the *right* colors, and can be as strong or as pale as you want them, go on perfectly, don't bleed or raise the grain.

CRAFTSMAN WOOD SERVICE CO.—2727 South Mary Street, Chicago, Illinois 60608

Send 50¢ for catalogue.

Like Constantine, this firm also supplies a complete line of cabinet woods and veneers and a basic line of everything else a cabinetmaking shop would need. Fewer hand tools than Constantine, but more power tools from the top makers—Stanley, Rockwell, Dremel, etc. Each of these houses is basic, but each catalogue carries things the other doesn't. Get both catalogues and buy your heavy things from the closest to you to avoid high shipping charges.

GASTON WOOD FINISHES—3630 East Tenth Street, Bloomington, Indiana 47401

Send 35¢ for catalogue.

This company specializes in taking the guesswork out of staining by supplying a set of color panels and directions how to mix their stains to match them. Lots of them, and the good colors and the hard ones interior decorators use. They sell no woods, but do have some fine reproductions of Victorian knobs, escutcheons, etc., that are hard to find. Also carved fruit drawer pulls in walnut, and antique clock faces and cases.

MOHAWK FINISHING PRODUCTS, INC.—Amsterdam, New York 12010

Send $2 for catalogue and colored wall chart.

As a basic supplier of the American furniture industry this company carries about 250 colors of stain soluble in alcohol or lacquer as standard stock, each available in powder form in small jars and usually sold in kits of 50 to furniture stores for use by their touch-up artist. Also about 150 colors of the burn-in or patching sticks (formerly known as shellac sticks) and these things are of course part of a complete system of finishing materials with which you can duplicate the surface of anything in the world that is hard. And their catalogues and literature explain in detail how everything is used. Their approach isn't to try to sell you anything—just to help you. But that doesn't include answering letters from amateurs. They are too busy selling their products by the gallon and drum.

You can spend hours reading their catalogue, because you are learning something every minute, and as far as I'm concerned their colored wall chart is the greatest work of art an antique restorer will ever see. All the stuff is there, and you just know that everything is possible if you just apply yourself. Obviously these stains and sticks can be and are used to restore a lot more than antique furniture—like Ming vases, Dresden china (there are over 20 whites), Aztec armor, Greek marble, and the mind boggles!

Incidentally, please be polite to these people as this is the first time they have sort of "gone public" with their catalogue and wall chart, and I don't want a lot of crazy cranks bothering them. Just send a brief note with your two dollars in it saying I sent you to them. When you do get their catalogue, the minimum order is $10, but you'd have to not care much about restoring antiques if that was all you spent with them.

FRAME REPAIRS

J & S ANTIQUE PRODUCTS—Box 4883, Chattanooga, Tennessee 37405

All kinds of instructions and materials related to ornate frames and old oil paintings. They make it easy to replace missing pieces, do gold leafing, clean varnish and restore oil paintings.

HERBERT A. JAPS—126 Seventh Ave., North, Hopkins, Illinois 55343

This company specializes in a wide variety of mouldings from which you can build complete frames. And for a slight charge will even send you four-inch long samples. They also sell liners of linen and velvet, matting and mat cutters that will cut oval or circular mats. Also small round and oval frames and touch up stuff.

LAMP PARTS

BROWN LAMP CO.—BOX 12511, Creve Coeur, Missouri 63141

These people have everything. Everything! Anything you can think of and stuff that would never occur to you in a million years. And they will sell you one piece at retail or if you want to start your own lamp store they will give you a shopping discount on wholesale orders.

MUSIC BOXES

WALTERS MODERN HOBBY SHOP—207 French Rd., Utica, N.Y. 13502

You wouldn't believe how many kinds of music box movements there are until you see this catalogue. And then they have about 300 tunes—which is every tine you can possibly think of putting in a music box. Plus disc movements and LP recordings of music box tunes.

STAINED GLASS

WHITMORE-DURGIN—BOX 2065, Hanover, Massachusetts 02339

When it comes to writing copy, these people are funnier than anybody else around. But they also have everything you need and lots of instructions with it for fixing stained glass lamp shades or windows. In fact, they will even sell you a form and put you in the business of making "antique" lamp shades from scratch. Don't laugh. I know a guy doing this and getting $400 a shade.

TOOLS

BROOKSTONE Co.—Peterborough, New Hampshire

This catalogue has got to be the most wonderful thing ever printed. These people have collected every conceivable hard to find tool in the world. Hundreds of them, and some of the damndest things. And if there are any women readers still with me, this is the perfect place to find presents for men. Whatever a man's interest, there's something in this catalogue he'd love to have.

VICTORIAN DRAWER PULLS

JOHNSON WOODCARVING Co.—1615 Delroy Avenue, Rockford, Illinois 61109

What this company has—and boy are they hard to find— are the carved wooden handles. They have five styles, and they come in either walnut or cherry. (For metal Victorian pulls—including the tear-drop ones—get the Horton Brasses catalogue listed above under *Brasses*.)

Index

Page numbers in italics indicate illustrations.